Women Psychotherapists' Reflections on Female Friendships

Psychologists, as well as the general public, have recognized the importance of female friendships. Scientists call this bond the tending instinct—a kind of female relaxation response that has salutary effects. Such special attachment shields women from isolation and provides an enhanced sense of wellbeing. Intimate friends can therefore act as sisters of the heart to promote connection, solace, wholeness, and longevity. Moreover, women friends frequently provide emotional, social, physical, and spiritual benefits. Indeed, sisters of the heart constitute an unparalleled bond that encourages women to connect with themselves, with others, and with the world at large. In this book, twelve women therapists, who are diverse in age—young, middle-aged, and older women—as well as in ethnicity—White, African American, Latina, Asian American, Native American, and multiracial women—examine the psychological and physical aspects of this unique female bonding. Through their narratives we hear their distinctive voices as women and as healers. In this fashion, they reflect on both the functional and dysfunctional dynamics occurring between intimate female friends. Finally, these women therapists examine how their experiences with a sister of the heart informed their development as healers, and discuss how they use this special bond in psychotherapy with women.

This book was originally published as a special issue of *Women & Therapy*.

This enlightening, iconic book is for anyone who wants to understand more about the powerful roles of friendships—including challenges—among women that facilitate their ability to survive and thrive. It is special in that the chapter authors are psychotherapists who describe the impact of female bonding, from scientific as well as personal bases. The descriptions are rooted in theory, research, extensive clinical experience and personal lives. Refreshing and much needed, this book will prove useful to professionals as well as any women or men who want to understand the value and salience of female relationships.

Melba Vasquez, Ph.D., ABPP
Past President, American Psychological Association
Independent Practice, Austin, Texas

Lillian Comas-Diaz, Ph.D., is a clinical psychologist in a private practice, and Clinical Professor at the George Washington University School of Medicine, USA. She is the author of over one hundred publications. Her recent books include: *Multicultural Care: A Clinician's Guide to Cultural Competence*; and *Women Psychotherapists: Journeys in Healing* (with M.B. Weiner).

Marcella Bakur Weiner, Ph.D., is a fellow of the American Psychological Association and has a doctorate in metaphysics/theology. She is author of 23 books and 75 articles. Her most recent books include: *Psychotherapy and Religion, Many Paths, One Journey*; and *Women Psychotherapists: Journeys in Healing* (with L. Comas-Diaz).

Women Psychotherapists' Reflections on Female Friendships

Sisters of the Heart

Edited by

Lillian Comas-Diaz and Marcella Bakur Weiner

Routledge
Taylor & Francis Group
LONDON AND NEW YORK

First published 2014
by Routledge
4 Park Square, Milton Park, Abingdon, Oxon, OX14 4RN

Simultaneously published in the USA and Canada
by Routledge
605 Third Avenue, New York, NY 10017

Routledge is an imprint of the Taylor & Francis Group, an informa business

British Library Cataloguing in Publication Data
A catalogue record for this book is available from the British Library

ISBN 13: 978-0-415-84226-6 (hbk)

Typeset in Garamond
by Taylor & Francis Books

Publisher's Note
The publisher accepts responsibility for any inconsistencies that may have arisen during the conversion of this book from journal articles to book chapters, namely the possible inclusion of journal terminology.

Disclaimer
Every effort has been made to contact copyright holders for their permission to reprint material in this book. The publishers would be grateful to hear from any copyright holder who is not here acknowledged and will undertake to rectify any errors or omissions in future editions of this book.

Contents

Citation Information

The following chapters were originally published in *Women & Therapy*, volume 36, issue 1–2 (January 2013). When citing this material, please use the original page numbering for each article, as follows:

Chapter 1
Sisters of the Heart: How Women's Friendships Heal
Lillian Comas-Diaz and Marcella Bakur Weiner
Women & Therapy, volume 36, issue 1–2 (January 2013) pp. 1–10

Chapter 2
Feminist Therapy as a Path to Friendship with Women
Laura S. Brown
Women & Therapy, volume 36, issue 1–2 (January 2013) pp. 11–22

Chapter 3
Acts of Remembering: Relationship in Feminist Therapy
Sherri Taylor
Women & Therapy, volume 36, issue 1–2 (January 2013) pp. 23–34

Chapter 4
Growing at the Hyphen: Female Friendships and Social Context
Pratyusha Tummala-Narra
Women & Therapy, volume 36, issue 1–2 (January 2013) pp. 35–50

Chapter 5
Hermanas de Corazón y Alma
Carrie L. Castañeda-Sound
Women & Therapy, volume 36, issue 1–2 (January 2013) pp. 51–61

Chapter 6
Comadres: The Healing Power of a Female Bond
Lillian Comas-Diaz
Women & Therapy, volume 36, issue 1–2 (January 2013) pp. 62–75

Chapter 7
A Complicated Friendship
Louise Bordeaux Silverstein
Women & Therapy, volume 36, issue 1–2 (January 2013) pp. 76–85

Chapter 8
Sisters of the Heart Along the Way: The Power of the Female Mentoring Relationship
Jennifer Ruff
Women & Therapy, volume 36, issue 1–2 (January 2013) pp. 86–99

Chapter 9
Sister of the Heart and Mind: Healing and Teaching with Family System Constellations
Janice Crawford
Women & Therapy, volume 36, issue 1–2 (January 2013) pp. 100–109

Chapter 10
Sister Friends: A Reflection and Analysis of the Therapeutic Role of Sisterhood in African American Women's Lives
Thema Bryant-Davis
Women & Therapy, volume 36, issue 1–2 (January 2013) pp. 110–120

Chapter 11
Awakening Resilience: Recovery Within Intimate Female Friendships
Iva GreyWolf
Women & Therapy, volume 36, issue 1–2 (January 2013) pp. 121–126

Chapter 12
Make New Friends but Keep the Old: The Sisterhood Bonds that Have Shaped Me
Michi Fu
Women & Therapy, volume 36, issue 1–2 (January 2013) pp. 127–138

Notes on Contributors

Laura S. Brown, Fremont Community Therapy Project, Seattle, Washington, USA.

Thema Bryant-Davis, Pepperdine University, Malibu, California, USA.

Carrie L. Castañeda-Sound, Pepperdine University, Encino, California, USA.

Lillian Comas-Diaz, Transcultural Mental Health Institute, Washington, DC, USA.

Janice Crawford, Private Practice, New York, USA.

Michi Fu, California School of Professional Psychology of Alliant International University and Asian Pacific Family Center of Pacific Clinics, Los Angeles, California, USA.

Iva GreyWolf, University of Alaska Fairbanks College of Rural & Community Development, Fairbanks, Alaska, USA; University of Alaska Southeast, Sitka, Alaska, USA.

Jennifer Ruff, University of California, San Francisco, California Department of Corrections and Rehabilitation, San Francisco, California, USA.

Louise Bordeaux Silverstein, Ferkauf Graduate School of Psychology, Yeshiva University, Bronx, New York, USA.

Sherri Taylor, The Wright Institute, Berkeley, California, USA.

Pratyusha Tummala-Narra, Boston College, Massachusetts, USA.

Marcella Bakur Weiner, Long Island University, Brooklyn, New York, USA.

Sisters of the Heart: How Women's Friendships Heal

LILLIAN COMAS-DIAZ
Transcultural Mental Health Institute, Washington, DC
MARCELLA BAKUR WEINER
Long Island University, Brooklyn, New York

In this article we focus on the healing aspects of women's intimate friendships with other women. In particular, we discuss the role of female neurohromone oxytocin "the love hormone" in the promotion of health and wellbeing among women. We assert that the intimate women friendship construct can enhance psychotherapy's healing and empowering functions. In this context, we examine how women's friendships can inform feminist psychotherapy. Moreover, we discuss the feminist therapeutic relationship as an intimate bond, and compare it with women's friendships. We conclude with the introduction of the special issue on "Sisters of the Heart: Women Psychotherapist Reflections on Female Friendships."

"We learn best to listen to our own voices if we are listening at the same time to other women--whose stories, for all our differences, turn out, if we listen well, to be our stories also."

– Barbara Deming

INTRODUCTION

Females tend to care for each other. The animal kingdom provides multiple illustrations of this phenomenon. For instance, female monkeys groom each other, lionesses breastfeed each other's cubs, and female elephants communicate with each other with their chums in a unique way through low-pitched vocalizations (Angier, 2012). Likewise, women's longing for female friends has ancient roots. While men hunted and women nurtured, females developed a special connection that helps them to cope in life.

We begin this anthology with a discussion of the role of female friendship in women's lives. Specifically, we examine the psychological and physical well-being aspects of female bonding. Since women's happiness is contagious (Stein, 2008), intimate female friendships enhance women's self-esteem, connectedness, and enjoyment. Indeed, research has documented that having intimate female friends throughout life promotes health and a sense of well-being (Knickmeyer, Sexton, & Nishimura, 2002). Simply put, women keep their friends healthy. Moreover, they provide emotional, social, physical, and spiritual benefits. Women friends even contribute to women's longevity. Contrary to men—who tend to live longer if they are married—women with intimate female friends live longer, regardless of marital status (Felder, 2006).

Indeed, relationships are the source of women's successful development and psychological health (Miller & Stiver, 1997). To illustrate, Jean Baker Miller (Miller & Stiver, 1997) argued that women's development occurs in connection, that is, within relationships that provide mutual empowerment and mutual empathy. Certainly, intimate female friends contribute to women's healing process.

HEALING AND WOMEN FRIENDSHIPS

The salutary effects of female bonding extend throughout the course of women's lives. First, having a sister is beneficial to her siblings' health (Tannen, 2010). Padilla-Walker and her colleagues (2010) studied a large number of families with at least two children. Results indicated that having a sister protected children from feeling lonely, depressed, guilty, unloved, self-conscious, and anxious. The researchers interpreted their findings through the lens of gender socialization. That is, they concluded that sisters tend to be better listeners, better at discussing problems, and better caretakers than brothers (Padilla-Walker et al., 2010).

Similarly, research found that having a best friend present during stressful events significantly protected children from the negative effects of such difficult experiences (Adams, Santo, & Bukowski, 2011). Based on these findings, we can infer that the presence of best friends reduces the negative effects of stressful situations among children. Moreover, research found that adolescent girls with intimate female friends had higher self-esteem, were better adjusted, and displayed superior coping than did those with less intimate friend relationships (Hartup & Stevens, 1999).

Following these research findings, we can surmise that women tend to offer security, refuge, hope and solace to their friends. What is more, female friends help to mark the stages of a woman's life. For instance, female milestones such as menstruation, pregnancy, and post partum rituals strengthen women's connection to each other. The ancient practice of the "red tent" may illustrate the social origins of women's bonding. Anita Diamant (1997) described how according to ancient law, women menstruating or giving birth retreated to a tent (hence, a red tent) to receive support and encouragement from their mothers, sisters, grandmothers, aunts, and other caretaking women.

As a matter of fact, women's special bonding has a biological component. Besides their socialization to become caretakers, women have a tending instinct—a kind of female relaxation response. The "tend and befriend" instinct is opposite to the fight or flight response. The tending instinct facilitates the release of oxytocin—an anti-stress neurohormone (Taylor, 2002). Originally known to stimulate labor, lactation, maternal behavior, and social bonding, oxytocin, plays an important role in promoting relaxation, healing, and sense of well-being (Uvnas-Moberg & Petersson, 2005). In short, this neurohormone enhances women's abilities to befriend, nurture, and heal. In its relaxation role and anxiolytic-like effect, oxytocin reduces blood pressure and cortisol (the stress hormone) levels in humans. To illustrate, in the previously mentioned research, Adams and colleagues (2011) reported that having a best friend present during stressful situations maintained children's levels of cortisol within normal levels.

In its health promotion role, oxytocin increases pain thresholds. Along these lines, repeated exposure to oxytocin causes long-lasting relaxation effects by influencing the activity of other transmitter systems (Uvnas-Moberg & Petersson, 2005).

Interestingly, research has shown that oxytocin exerts a positive role in social attachment (Boultet et al., 2006). Since oxytocin increases prosocial behavior, this neurohormone can potentially promote positive social interactions. To illustrate, Jesso and colleagues (2011) found that the administration of intranasal oxytocin resulted in a reduction of the recognition of angry faces among patients with behavioral variant frontotemporal dementia. These research findings show that oxytocin is an important mediator of social behavior and suggest that oxytocin can be a potential treatment for attachment problems. Furthermore, while a positive environment continuously activates oxytocin, psychological mechanisms such as positive interactions involving touch and support, trigger the release of oxytocin in a health-promoting way (Uvnas-Moberg & Petersson, 2005). Additionally, psychological mechanism such as warmth and empathy may trigger the release of oxytocin (Uvnas-Moberg & Petersson, 2005). In other words, various types of psychotherapy involving the transfer of support, warmth, empathy, and connectedness—such as feminist therapy—can promote health.

Without a doubt, women's tending instinct, facilitated by oxytocin (the "love" hormone), shields women from isolation, facilitates functional coping, and promotes healing. Certainly, women foster their friends' health, well-being, and happiness. In this way, the articles in this anthology illustrate the role female friendships have in feminist psychotherapy with women.

WOMEN FRIENDSHIPS AND PSYCHOTHERAPY

Since women connect with each other in a special way to provide support, relaxation, and healing, it is not surprising that literary women authors have recognized the benefits of women's friendships. For example, in her memoir "Truth and Beauty: A Friendship," Ann Pachett (2004) portrayed her intimate friendship with Lucinda M. Grealy as" being family without being bound by blood," and sharing a "love for the rest of her life without being romantic partners." Likewise, Lisa See (2005) in her novel "Snow Flower and the Secret Fan," narrated the story of two Chinese friends who became "laotong" or sworn sisters, and consequently, developed a secret language (*Nu shun*) to communicate solely between themselves.

Consistent with these notions, there are multiple terms to designate intimate female friends. Some designations include sister-friends, *comadres* (co-mothers, allomothers), sworn sisters, *hermanas del alma*, (sisters of the soul), among many others. We adopted Chitra Banerjee Divakanuri's (2000) term from her novel "Sister of My Heart," to designate intimate women's friendships in this collection. Moreover, different ways to depict an intimate woman friend abound in the popular lore. For instance, a close woman friend can be described as "someone you can be yourself with; someone you can trust; someone you can call at 4:00 AM; someone you know for a long time; someone who understands you; among many other operational definitions. We believe that the concept "sisters of the heart" includes all of the previously mentioned descriptions—and even more. Sisters of the heart constitute an unparalleled supportive bond that encourages women to navigate joys and sorrows, in order to promote connection, support, healing, and growth.

In this context, "Sisters of the Heart: Women Psychotherapists' Reflections on Female Friendships" describes the special bond between intimate women friends and its healing and transformative power. Therapists or not, most women treasure their close sisterly friendships and recognize their transformative power. Indeed, feminist scholars have described how women's friendships provide an impetus for social change (Castaneda & Burns-Glover, 2008). Likewise, the empowering healing of women friendships has inspired this anthology's contributors.

To explore how intimate female friends foster meaning, connection, and wellbeing, we asked women therapists to narrate their experience with female bonding. First, we invited feminist therapists to reflect on how their intimate female friendships shaped them. Then, we asked them to examine how their intimate women friendship informed their professional development as therapists. Finally, we solicited their reflections on the role of intimate women friendships in feminist therapy. In this way, the essays in "Sisters of the Heart" analyze the significance, nature, depth, and challenges of close female connection.

FEMINIST THERAPEUTIC RELATIONSHIPS AND INTIMATE FRIENDSHIPS

The feminist therapeutic relationship and an intimate friendship are related. Even though psychotherapists and their clients are not friends, the feminist therapeutic relationship shares characteristics with a close female friendship. For instance, both relationships involve the development of intimate emotional bonds between women. In this fashion, feminist therapists promote connectedness, empowerment, healing, and transformation. Similar to close women friends, feminist therapists foster self-nurturing as a form of empowerment.

A main difference, however, is that the client's wellbeing takes center stage in feminist psychotherapy (Feminist Therapy Institute, 1990, 2008). To promote this goal, therapists foster self-empathy and help clients to reconnect with their strengths during psychotherapy. Moreover, feminist therapists offer support, validation, and understanding of their clients' reality. They encourage clients to become critically aware of their oppressive circumstances (Feminist Therapy Institute, 1990, 2008). Although the feminist therapeutic relationship is not as reciprocal as a close friendship, it is infused with mutuality (Enns, 2000). In other words, the feminist therapist uses her tending instinct for mutual empowerment. She "gives" (Sue & Zane, 1987) by acknowledging her client's multiple intersecting identities and gender specific sociocultural contexts (Comas-Diaz, 2012). And yet, she "receives" by tending and caring for her client—as well as for herself. Even though feminist psychotherapeutic tenets acknowledge the power inequality between therapist and client, the feminist healing relationship aims to be egalitarian and non-hierarchical (Brown, 2010). Notwithstanding the feminist equality foundation, the therapist holds accountability for empowering her client (Feminist Therapy Institute, 1990, 2008). Indeed, an aspect of this accountability is the therapist's cognitive and affective "presence" in her client's life. Similar to an intimate friendship—where a close woman friend listens and witnesses her friend's stories—the feminist therapist bears witness to her client's story of distress. In this process, she helps clients to recover their voices and to re-author their life stories.

WOMEN TELLING STORIES: MENDING HEARTS AND HEALING LIVES

"Story is far older than the art of science and psychology, and will always be the elder in the equation no matter how much time passes." – Clarissa Pinkola Estes

Telling stories lead to women's healing and empowerment (Anderson & Jack, 1991). Indeed, storytelling can be life-saving and a reason for living (Kay, 1998). Indeed, as a therapeutic technique, storytelling facilitates women's integration of fragmented experiences (Aron, 1992; Cienfuegos & Monelli, 1983). Moreover, storytelling opens up a testimonial space that helps women to reconnect with a sense of purpose and effectiveness through helping others (Fischman & Ross, 1990). Likewise, the contributors in this collection use their unique voices, as both women and therapists, to tell their stories. They reflect upon how diverse types of intimate female relationships such as teachers, mentors, colleagues, employees, relatives, and even historical role models became sisters of their heart. Many therapists chose a nurturing mother–daughter bond as a template to inform their intimate female friendships.

As women's gender related experiences are situated in a stratified and hierarchical society (Jordan, 2010), the contributors recognize that women's realities intersect with gender, ethnicity, race, socioeconomic status, age, religion/spirituality, and other diversity variables. In a similar fashion, the therapists in this anthology come from different walks of life. They are young, middle-aged, and older women; as well as White, African American, Latina, Asian American, Native American, and multiracial women. Additionally, these feminist therapists endorse diverse types of spirituality/religion, ranging from Judaism, Christianity, Hinduism, Buddhism, and or spiritual syncretism.

As editors of this collection, we identified two major areas to facilitate the unfolding of the contributors' stories. These areas include contributors' personal female relationships, and the friendships' impact on how they conduct psychotherapy with women. In particular, the therapists discuss feelings evoked in feminist therapy regarding female friendships—including psychological processes such as transference/countertransference, identification, trust conflict, and mutual empowerment. Moreover, most of the women therapists provide clinical material illustrating the role of intimate women relationships in the practice of feminist therapy. Finally, "Sisters of the Heart: Women Psychotherapist Reflections on Female Friendships" allows for diverse therapists' voices to articulate a wealth of wisdom that readers can resonate with. They offer lessons learned and suggestions for therapists, as well as for women clients.

The women therapists not only comment on the dynamics between intimate female friends, but also on the nature of their bonding. Their stories elucidate the essence of intimate women friendships. For instance, Laura S. Brown explores feminist therapy as a path for friendships among women. Aided by feminist principles, she discusses how she transformed her childhood and adolescent experiences of relational aggression into a deepened understanding of the value and importance of relationships between women.

Sherri Taylor, an African American young woman, identifies lesbian feminist of color Audre Lorde, as a sister of her heart. She offers lessons to feminist therapists based on Lorde's work. Taylor's lessons center in the feminist psychotherapy relationship and include the therapeutic alliance, transference/countertransference, work with women's embodied experience, and endorsement of cultural competence.

Next, Pratyusha Tummala-Narra identifies women's friendships as important sources of support for immigrant women. She explores the development of friendship in the context of immigration and cultural adaptation. Most importantly, Tummala-Narra discussess how female friendships help women immigrant's development through the negotiation of a hyphenated identity. Likewise, Carrie L. Castañeda-Sound describes how her *hermana de corazón y alma* (sister of her heart and soul) helped her develop a mestiza consciousness during childhood and adolescence. Moreover, Castañeda-Sound discusses how the friendship influenced the development of her cultural identity and her professional role as a Chicana feminist therapist.

Lillian Comas-Diaz discusses how she reconnected with her healing legacy while coping with transculturation. She narrates the story of her relationship with her sister of the heart as a source of encouragement, sustenance and healing. Based on this relationship Comas-Diaz proposes the use of *comadre* (or allomother) therapy as a cultural and gender specific feminist therapy. She presents a case study illustrating a *mujerista* (Latina feminism) therapy.

Working within a *comadre* paradigm, Louise Bordeaux Silverstein raises a poignant issue within feminist theory. She discusses how an unequal power relationship evolved into an intimate friendship. She describes her relationship with an immigrant woman who helped take care of her children, to later become her *comadre* or allomother. Silverstein offers powerful lessons regarding the interaction of gender, immigration, poverty, and acculturation in women's lives.

Jennifer Ruff presents another "unequal" power relationship in the development of a sister of the heart bond. She shares her experience as a woman student and early career psychologist in the context of her relationship with a woman mentor. Ruff identifies support, modeling, transparency, and spiritual connectedness as important characteristics of her mentoring relationship, as well as intimate women friendships. Likewise, Janice Crawford illustrates how a teacher–student relationship became a "sister of the heart" connection. She discusses the teachings of a practitioner of Hellinger's systemic family constellation therapy and the empowering impact on her relationships with women, as well as on her psychotherapeutic practice.

Next, Thema Bryant-Davis discusses ethnically diverse women's sisters of their heart. She documents the healing effects of friendship among African American women. She examines how Sister friends help African American women to cope with stress and trauma. Moreover, Bryant-Davis discusses a case study of an African American woman in need of mutual sister friends through a womanist psychological perspective

Iva GreyWolf discusses the effects of oppression on American Indian women friendships. Since the lives of many Native American women are fraught with violence and trauma, there is a pressing need to develop theories and practices that focus on the intersection of state, colonial and gender violence for this women population (Smith, 2005). Iva GreyWolf's story highlights these issues as she articulates the challenges—including horizontal aggression—within close friendships when women internalize their oppression. Her story demonstrates the effect of a betrayal in an intimate friendship—a situation that paradoxically helped her to recover from co-dependency and reconnect with resilience.

Finally, Michi Fu discusses the developmental relevance of women friendships throughout the course of women's lives. By exhorting readers to "make new friends, but keep the old," Fu illustrates how female friends have helped her develop a woman-centered therapeutic style.

CONCLUSION: "WOMEN GIVE BIRTH WITH OTHER WOMEN"

Women's intimate friendships are a source of support, sustenance and healing. Indeed, women have befriended women since the beginning of time. The African proverb: "Women give birth with other women " is a testament to the power of female bonding. Definitely, the therapists in this anthology demonstrate how feminist therapy helps women to give psychological birth to themselves in the company of other women. Finally, the narratives in this compilation show how sisters of the heart can improve women's psychological health and sense of wellbeing. They suggest that feminist psychotherapy is best equipped to address the relational needs of women, as well as to capitalize on the benefits of women's connectedness and healing abilities.

REFERENCES

Adams, R. E., Santo, J.B., & Bukowski, W. M. (2011, November). The presence of a best friend buffers the effects of negative experiences. *Developmental Psychology, 47*(6), 1786–1791.

Anderson, K., & Jack, D. C. (1991). Learning to listen: Interviews techniques and analyses. In S. B. Gluck & D. Patai (Eds.), *Women's worlds: The feminist practice of oral history.* New York, London: Routledge.

Angier, N. (2012, April 23). The spirit of sisterhood is in the air and on the air. *The New York Times*, Science section. Retrieved on April 24, 2012 from: http://www.nytimes.com/2012/04/24/science/how-hbos-girls-mirrors-the-spirit-of-sisterhood-in-nature.html?pagewanted=2&_r=1&ref=science

Aron, A. (1992). Testimonio, a bridge between psychotherapy and sociotherapy. *Women & Therapy, 13*(3), 173–189.

Boultet, C., Vercuell, L., Schelestraete, C., Buffin, A., & Legros, J. J. (2006). Oxytocin and maternal stress during post partum period (Abstract). *Annals of Endocrinology (Paris), 67*(3), 214–223.

Brown, L. S. (2010). *Feminist therapy.* Theories of Psychotherapy Series. Washington, DC: American Psychological Association.

Castaneda, D., & Burns-Glover, A. (2008). Women's friendships and romantic relationships. In F. Denmark & M. Paludi (Eds.), *Psychology of Women: A handbook of issues and theories*. Second edition. Westport, CT: Praeger.

Cienfuegos, A. J., & Moneli, C. (1983). The testimony of political repression as a therapeutic instrument. *American Journal of Orthopsychiatry, 53*, 43–51.

Comas-Diaz, L. (2012). *Multicultural care: A clinician's guide to cultural competence.* Washington, DC: American Psychological Association.

Diamant, A. (1997). *The red tent.* New York: St Martins Press.

Divakanuri, C. B. (2000). *Sister of my heart: A novel.* New York: Anchor Books.

Enns, C. (2000). Gender issues in counseling. In S. D. Brown & R. W. Lent (Eds.), *Handbook of counseling psychology* (3rd edition) (pp. 601-638). Hoboken, NJ: Wiley & Sons.

Felder, S. (2006). The gender longevity gap: Explaining the difference between singles and couples. *Journal of Population Economics, 19*(3), 543–557.

Feminist Therapy Institute (1990). Feminist Therapy Institute Code of Ethics. In H. Lerman & N. Porter (Eds.), *Feminist ethics in psychotherapy* (pp. 37–40). New York: Springer.

Feminist Therapy Institute (2000). Feminist therapy code of ethics. Denver, CO: Author.

Finger, E.C. (2011). The effects of oxytocin on social cognition and behaviour in frontotemporal dementia. *Brain, 134*, 2493–2501.

Fishman, Y., & Ross, J. (1990). Group treatment of exiled survivors of torture. *American Journal of Orthopsychiatry, 60*, 135–142.

Hartup, W. W., & Stevens, N. (1999). Friendships and population across the life span. *Current Directions in Psychological Science, 8*, 76–79.

Jesso, S., Morlog, D., Ross, S., Pell, M. D., Pasternak, S. H., Mitchell, D. G. V., Kertesz, A., Knickmeyer, N., Sexton, K., & Nishimura, N. (2002). The impact of same-sex friendships on the well-being of women: A review of the literature. *Women & Therapy, 25*(1), 37–59.

Jordan, J. V. (2010). *Relational-cultural therapy.* Theories of Psychotherapy Series. Washington, DC: American Psychological Association.

Kay, A. (1998). Generativity in the shadow of genocide: The Holocaust experience and generativity. In D. P. McAdams & E. de St. Aubin (Eds.), *Generativity and adult development: How and why we care for the next generation* (pp. 335–359). Washington, DC: American Psychological Association.

Miller, J. B., & Stiver, I. P. (1997). *The healing connection: How women form relationships in therapy and in life.* Boston: Beacon Press.

Patchett, A. (2004) *Truth and beauty: A friendship*. New York: HarperCollins Publishers.

Stein, R. (2008). Happiness can spread among people like a contagion, study indicates. *The Washington Post*, December 5, A 08.

Tannen, D. (2010). Why sisterly chats make people happier. The New York Times, November 6, retrieved from http://www.nytimes.com/2010/10/26/health/26essay.html

Taylor, S. E. (2002). *The tending instinct: How nurturing is essential to who we are and how we live*. New York: Holt.

See, L. (2005). *Snow flower and the secret fan*. New York: Random House.

Smith, A. (2005). Native American feminism, Sovereignty, and social change. *Feminist Studies*, *31*(1), 116–132.

Sue, S., & Zane, N. (1987). The role of culture and cultural techniques in psychotherapy. A critique and reformulation. *American Psychologist*, *55*, 37–45.

Uvnas-Moberg, K., & Petersson, M. (2005). Oxytocin, a mediator of anti-stress, well-being, social interaction, growth and healing (Abstract). *Z Psychosomatic Medical Psychotherapy*, *5*(1), 57–80.

Feminist Therapy as a Path to Friendship with Women

LAURA S. BROWN

Fremont Community Therapy Project, Seattle, Washington

While many feminist therapists have found that their personal experiences of friendship have given them an experiential base from which to develop their work, some feminist therapists have had alternative journeys through connections with women. This article explores how the author transformed her childhood and adolescent experiences of relational aggression into a deepened understanding of the value and importance of relationships between women. The contributions of misogyny and sexism to relational aggression among girls and women, and their enduring effects on all women's relationships to other women is explored. Finally, the author describes her intimate e-epistolary friendship with two other women, and considers how the medium of email and other forms of electronic communication may facilitate emotional intimacy for women who have experienced relational aggression with other women.

I have written more than a hundred pieces for professional journals in the last thirty years. Usually I can sit at the computer and, with an idea almost fully formed in my head, bat out a piece in an intensive day of work.

This article proves an exception to that norm. I have been wrestling with it for months, had multiple false starts with the electronic equivalent of crumpling the sheet of paper and throwing it into the recycle bin, sat at the keyboard feeling stumped and clueless. After months of struggling with this topic I have finally had light shine on my dilemma. My "aha" moment is this. I was tasked by the co-editors with writing a piece about how an intimate friendship with another woman has informed my development as a feminist therapist. But I can't respond to that request and tell the truth. Friendships with other women and girls had little or nothing to do with my becoming a feminist therapist, or with how I understand the work of feminist therapy. Rather, becoming a feminist therapist and writing about its theory and practice are what have taught me to value women, and to have deep and meaningful friendships with other women. It's difficult to know if I would have had women friends had I never become a feminist, and thus a feminist therapist. Why this is so, and how feminism and feminist therapy allowed me to develop the rich and loving network of women friends who enhance my life today, is what this article is about.

Becoming a feminist gave me the intellectual context in which I was nourished to do my work and develop feminist therapy theory and practice. Had I been waiting to have women friends in my life before becoming a feminist therapist I would have been entirely absent from this topic with which I have become so professionally identified (Brown, 1994, 2009). My understanding of friendship, which was a tentative and at times anxious experience for me during the first two decades of my life, was informed powerfully by my participation in the women's movement and my becoming a feminist therapist. For me, the directionality of the relationship is opposite to that posited by the editors.

In some ways I am fortunate in having had a dearth of female friends in my earlier years. I have had few bad habits in relationships with women to confront and correct. Never having participated much in the normal rituals of girls' and women's relationships before feminism, I skipped the stage of development where you abandon your best friend for the boy/man you are dating, for instance, or join a cliques that excludes other girls/women.

What I do have, and what has informed me greatly as a therapist, are the memories of having been, for most of my childhood and adolescence, the odd girl out, the one on the other end of those problematic patterns of same-sex peer relationships that grow in the toxic soil of patriarchal and misogynist societies. That odd girl inside of me has been a deep source of knowing about how to create the space of feminist therapy. Ironically, the absence of same-sex friendships in my early years has also informed my theory and practice by giving me a particular type of experiential data regarding the power and value of connections between women.

Had I never become a feminist I would likely have remained the girl and young woman I was, having few if any deep friendships with other girls and women, feeling alien to the rituals and realities of conventional womanhood. As a child and adolescent I spent time socially with boys and men, where I felt more comfortable and at home. Boys and men were easy to deal with; they wanted to do projects, talk about science or politics, or put on musicals. I relished being told by many of my male peers that I was not like other girls. I was a father's daughter, in a family where gender was only lightly noted. My family encouraged to participate in the sciences, which is where the boys were. I did not like girls who, for the most part, seemed to dislike me.

When I became a feminist I was able to see how I had internalized sexist attitudes and norms about women, particularly misogynist contempt and disdain for women's interest in beauty and personal appearance, both of which my mother herself devalued. A component of my outsider-girl status had to do with my lack of empathy for or interest in that entire sphere of life, a stance that was highly valued at home. While much of this eschewal of the entire topic of fashion, beauty and appearance was, as I can see in retrospect, a self-protective strategy for dealing with being on the outside from other girls and young women, it taught me to devalue aspects of Euro-American culture's stereotypic tropes of femininity that I have struggled to like and appreciate in myself and other women over time.

I have those boys and men of my childhood and adolescence, particularly those who I worked with in the anti-war movement of the late 1960s, to thank for having helped to raise my consciousness and transform me into a feminist. They taught me to expect to be taken seriously for my intellect and political contributions. Because I had not internalized the sexist notion that I, as a female, had lesser intellectual capacities than my male peers, I could hold my own in debate, and believed that my ideas were worth being listened to. But then these same comrades turned around and acted as if most women weren't worth being respected in the ways they seemed to respect and include me. The injustice and unfairness of that stance—I was the exceptional woman, others were "chicks" to be used as sexual playmates and ornamentation—propelled me into the women's movement. Because of my strange relationship with sexism, and my being identified as a father's daughter/female son in the world, I was shocked when I became its target.

The moment of my conversion to feminism is crystal clear. I began to take women seriously in January, 1971 in Madison Wisconsin, when a room full of young men in a radical left movement in which I was a campus organizer decided that they were unwilling to add a vote of support for women's liberation to the long list of national liberation movements with which our group was voting solidarity. Women, they said jokingly, did not need liberating, except perhaps from their unwillingness to be as sexually available as the boy-men in the room wished them to be. I was one of two female campus organizers in the room; the two of us, and the four or five women there as "chicks," the women on the arm of their organizer boyfriends, became angry, and decamped in a cloud of derision to a separate room. There we ventilated our rage at what had just occurred, and considered how we might support one another. Instead of feeling threatened by the "chicks," who had seemed on first glance to be the grown-up version of the girls who had been excluding me forever, I felt connected to them as sisters who were suffering from the same injustice as I was. For the first time that I could recall, at the age of 18, I had serious conversations with other women, and liked it. I left that meeting a budding feminist. When I returned to my college campus I found the women's liberation movement on campus, and have never looked back.

Becoming a feminist made me sit up and pay attention to other women for the first time. This in turn made it impossible for me to avoid noticing my sexual and romantic feelings toward them. As a feminist therapist who has now worked with many lesbians of my age cohort who struggled through the difficulties of acknowledging their sexualities I can see that my distance from girls and women in adolescence was socially protective, allowing me to escape the experience of homophobia during more vulnerable stages of my personal development. The girls and young women among my peers who could not suppress that erotic knowing suffered terribly; I benefited in my lesbian identity development by not coming out until I had the protective factor of feminism to buffer homophobia in the larger culture.

Becoming a feminist also allowed me to believe that friendships with women might be possible for me. Such relationships had not been part of my life until then. Friendship and relationships with other girls and women are long-standing areas of difficulty for me. I have always had a difficult and arm's length relationship with my mother. She liked other women well enough, and had close women friends whose families related to mine when I was growing up. But she did not particularly like me, although she did her level best to encourage and support my intellectual development. I annoyed most of my women teachers by being gender non-conforming to one degree or another. The ones who I can now look back on and read as lesbian were the most uncomfortable, and worked the hardest to herd me into the precincts of conventional femininity, which only led to more conflict and distance. With the wisdom of hindsight I can appreciate that they were doing their best to protect me, and likely every other girl who triggered their "gaydar." The concept of relational aggression among girls had not yet been developed when I was preadolescent and adolescent (Lamb, 2002), but when I first read about it I recognized my own experiences with other girls quite clearly.

WHAT NON-FRIENDSHIP WITH WOMEN TAUGHT ME

I was an odd, quirky little girl. I spouted facts (leading to the predictable nickname of Encyclopedia), refused to like the Beatles until Rubber Soul, sang opera in the school hallways, and dressed a little strangely until I was old enough to make my own clothing. There were other girls who I liked and yearned to have choose me as a friend, but in nearly every social setting in which I participated—school, Hebrew school, girl scouts, choirs, the anti-war movement—I was the odd girl out, the one picked last after last. My relationships with boys were more pleasant, particularly with those who in retrospect I can predict likely grew up to be gay men and who were part of the musical theater world with me in my adolescence. I have two younger brothers, who were then and continue to be my friends, so I knew how to be friends with boys and men. I was closer to my father than to my mother, and intellectually stimulated by him to participate in science fairs and compete with boys as intellectual equals.

When the looming presence of my 40th high school reunion put me electronically back in touch with people from my high school class I was surprised at how few names I recognized. I reached out to a few people who I had thought of as friends then—no response, which was no surprise. Those relationships were only about a millimeter deep, and none of them had survived my early departure from high school. Leaving high school after 11th grade was partially motivated by the social discomfort of the whole enterprise of being in high school. I had hoped that, once in college, I would be a better fit, which indeed became more true, especially after my consciousness was raised. I'm fairly certain that my adolescent confusion about sexuality—I never did quite get what it was that most of the other girls were seeing in boys, although I gave it a good try—had something to do with the fact that it was hard to recognize sexual attraction to girls when I barely ever spent time with them. But this sexual energy was likely present, and probably uncomfortable and confusing for the few other girls with whom I tried to hang out—all girls who have gone on to get married to men, according to the personal information posted on the high school reunion website.

The absence of experience of friendships with other girls and young women until the end of my adolescence taught me a great deal about the meanings and realities of being an outsider, about being stigmatized and lonely. It taught me about the powerful effects of social support, or its absence, and about the ways in which stigma can become internalized and reenacted relationally. It helped me to understand how capacities to trust can be affected, and how a person feeling desperate for connection may fail to honor her own boundaries and values. Thus, non-friendships with girls and women in my first two decades have created empathy in me for the complexities of relational wounding and the power of such wounds to engender emotional imbalance.

FEMINISM CHANGES MY COURSE

Becoming a feminist at age 18 changed the entire direction of my life. I had known since I was nine that I wanted to become a psychotherapist. Feminism quickly led me to the work of Phyllis Chesler (1972) and Naomi Weisstein (1970). Reading their critiques of psychology and psychotherapy nearly derailed me from my professional goals. I was in luck, though, Feminism made me critical of psychology and the entire project of so-called mental health. Feminism also got me into a consciousness-raising group. I'm not sure that I can call the women in that group my friends, as none of the relationships persisted, but they were the closest thing to friends that I had experienced at that point in my life.

Many of the women in my CR group were themselves already psychotherapists or on the path to their advanced degrees. Some of us had experienced the misogynist practices that Chesler documented, as professionals or patients or both. Most of them were also reading Chesler and Weisstein; several of us went together to hear Chesler speak in 1973 when she came through Cleveland, and one of our CR group members, a psychiatrist, hosted a reception at her home for this feminist psychology rockstar.

So my CR group friends became a sounding board for me of a sort I'd not previously had. In the moments when I thought that the sexism of psychology would require my abandoning my career dreams and goals, my CR group members encouraged me to submit a second round of grad school applications. They gave me my first lesson in the value of social support and female solidarity. They taught me that me about the careful dance of having one foot in the mainstream and one firmly planted in my own radical perspectives. They offered me mentoring from the standpoint of their relatively greater age and experience. One of my CR group members (and I am sad that I cannot remember who) told me that I of course had to get my doctorate, because I had ideas that it was important to have be heard. "People will listen to Dr. Brown," she said, "when they wouldn't give Laura the time of day." My first female mentor was that woman in my CR group.

Another member of that CR group was the person who introduced me to the Association for Women in Psychology. AWP was, in 1973, *the* place where radical feminist politics and psychology converged. It was at the very first AWP Conference in Fort Wayne Indiana in October of 1973 that I met my first self-identified feminist psychologists—and, more importantly, the first women calling themselves feminist therapists. I had come home.

THERAPY AND FRIENDSHIP—PARALLEL DANCES

Becoming a feminist therapist, and in the process having to deepen my understanding of what created heart-to-heart connections with others, created in me the interpersonal skills and capacities that made it possible for me to act as a friend toward other women. As I often tell trainees, friendship and psychotherapy have elements in common. They require mutual willingness to be open-hearted, to take emotional risks and to engender trust in one another. Importantly, psychotherapy is not a relationship of equality of power, but rather one where the therapist has ultimate responsibility for the boundaries of the relationship, and a primary commitment to the welfare of clients.

Equally importantly, neither in some ways is a friendship between women a truly equal one. Women come together as friends from the locations of our multiple and intersecting identities. We carry into our friendships with one another the power imbalances of those components of identity. My legally married heterosexual and bisexual women friends have privilege that I do not; my Euro-American heritage creates social ease that is denied to my women friends of color. Our lives are not equivalent; and as in feminist therapy, we value one another's lives in friendship equal one to the other.

Too, we bring to friendship, as we do to therapy, our fears of rejection, our past experiences of trust betrayed by other women. While this is not quite the transferential symbolic relationship inherent in psychotherapy, friendships between women are not simply about the manifest content of the relationship any more than psychotherapy is. Becoming a therapist taught me the skills with which to navigate the sometimes-stormy waters of friendships with women because it taught me how to swim in those deeps in my work. It has allowed me to know what it means to be the party with more power in the relationship; I have, in turn, drawn on my experience as the less powerful party to see the subtle and complex ways in which powerlessness affects my clients in the therapeutic relationship itself, and thus empower them.

Finally, becoming a feminist therapist put me in the path of the women who have become my friends. My oldest friends are women I met in graduate school and on my internship. My image of myself as a friend in those years is still somewhat distorted through the lens of my earlier experiences. It took a recent Facebook exchange with one of those women to be confronted with her view of me as someone who she, and many other women in our mutual lives, knew she could rely on implicitly for support, material and emotional. She also reminded me of a period when, confined to bed by a bad encounter between my eyes and the chlorine in a new pool, she and several other women in our grad school women's group brought me food from the burger joint and took me to doctor appointments until I could see and drive myself again. That message opened up a flood of lovely memories of the women whose lives became part of mine in graduate school, where I was finally not the odd girl out, but a loved and valued member of a sisterhood.

THE STATE OF FRIENDSHIP TODAY—AND HOW IT INFORMS MY WORK

Since some time in 1995 I have been in an email exchange with two women friends. We write at least once a day, almost every day. When one of us is away from her computer the other two continue the exchange, knowing that our absent member will read what's been written when she returns and reenter the joint fabric of our lives.

Our friendship is not an obvious one. We are superficially very different from one another; different ethnic backgrounds, different sexual orientations. Each of them is a committed parent, while I have never wanted children. All three of us hold doctorates in psychology, in widely divergent subspecialties. One of us likes to drink margaritas and watch football; one of us is happiest hiking in the wilderness and spending quiet time with her family. We see one another in person too rarely; we have only been in the same physical space together as a threesome perhaps five times in the 16 years of this relationship. The AWP Conference, where I first became a feminist therapist, has been the site of most of those meetings over the years, highlighting the importance of that organization in my personal life and development. If you ask me who are my closest friends, who are the women who know more of the details, hard and good of my life, whose lives I know the most intimately and with the most depth, I would instantly call out the names of these two beloved women. It was because of them and our friendship that I decided to write this article.

I have close friends here at home, friends who are loyal, loving, good playmates, people with whom I go out to dinner, go on walks, practice aikido. Yet contrary to the notion that the heart opens best when face-to-face, it is my two e-mail sisters, the women with whom I have shared my heart every day for a decade and a half and more, with whom I am the most intimate. Our bond, which was forged in the fires of a professional controversy that touched each of our lives in a personal and powerful way, has transcended the early topic of that connection to become, at least for me, the important emotional core of my daily life.

This friendship, which crosses boundaries and miles, has taught me lessons that I have brought into my work as a therapist repeatedly. One of the wounds that many women deal with, whether they are aware of it or not, is that due to relational aggression from other women and girls (Crick & Rose, 2000; Hadley, 2003).

Relational aggression is a topic that has only recently come under scrutiny. Sexism itself obscured this phenomenon, as relational aggression does not involve physical violence. Rather, it appears in such forms as shunning, the spreading of rumors, and exclusion in relational contexts among and between women and girls.

Many, if not most, women and girls have experiences of relational aggression, and many also have perpetrated it; thus, the topic carries shame, with victims having internalized self-blame, and perpetrators struggling to own this aspect of self. Some commentators have suggested that because, in dominant cultures in the U.S., more overtly aggressive behaviors by girls are stigmatized, they turn to relationally aggressive behaviors, which are considered gender-normative, when attempting to deal with feelings of anger and hurt toward others. While empirical research on this phenomenon has not shown meaningful sex differences in rates of relational aggression, girls and women report feeling more harmed by it psychologically.

Because of the ways in which all women internalize sexist and misogynist messages about one another, horizontal hostility has frequently been a strategy that women use with one another to maintain a sense of value. Thus, relational aggression between girls and women nearly always includes components of gendered stereotypes regarding what in a particular female person is valuable. If I am somehow better than other women—less adherent to devalued female stereotypes, e.g., more science-and-math-minded, or more adherent to valued ones, e.g., more conventionally attractive to men—then I have a means by which to see myself as worthwhile without having to directly address the dynamics of sexism in my own life. If I ascribe gendered devalued attributes to another girl or woman, e.g., that she is sexually free (aka "a slut"), that she is not a critical thinker ("dumb blonde"), that she is overly masculine (a lesbian), I am assuring my own place in the hierarchy without ever challenging or questioning the misogyny erecting that stratified structure of value and worth for women.

I utilize this knowledge when working with women clients by asking questions that illuminate the manners in which such sexist tropes have affected their relationships with self and other women. Reframing problematic interactions with other women in terms of the wounds of internalized sexism and misogyny disrupts the "You cannot trust other women" narrative that is prevalent among so many women. The notion that women's solidarity with one another threatens larger cultural structures is both a new awareness for many women, and an empowering frame into which they can put their past struggles.

This kind of horizontal hostility among women seems, in my experience as a therapist, especially common in the lives of women who have been victimized by men; one of the ways in which they have become unable to obtain social support and a sense of sisterhood with women who have had similar experiences emerges in their narratives of female exceptionality ("I'm not like other women") and relational aggression ("Other women don't like me, and I can't trust them"). Unpacking this discourse of internalized misogyny, and noting how it has rendered a woman more vulnerable to intimate violence and victimization, creates options for self-empowerment as these clients learn, as I did, that women can be their friends, and more importantly, the sources of their personal power and safety.

THE POWER OF THE EPISTOLARY RELATIONSHIP

In preparing to write this essay about the impact of my friendships with other women on my work as a feminist therapist, I've thought long and deeply about how it is that my most intimate connections in adult life have often occurred at a distance rather than in person, and what this implies for the applications of the lessons of friendship to the work of psychotherapy. The sister-friends who called me on my 50th birthday live thousands of miles and three times zones from me. While our initial in-person connections with one another were immediate, these relationships are perforce almost entirely conducted at the keyboards of our computers, and seem unaffected by the gaps of time and space that occur between our perhaps-yearly encounters with one another at psychology conventions. My relationship with my partner began on-line, and deepened there, moving from an ambivalent dating relationship to being deeply in love during daily on-line chats while I was working out of the country for two months and we could only meet on-line. The epistolary relationship, which seems to be a relic of times gone by, has been a hallmark of many of my most powerful intimate connections with other women in my adulthood.

Why might this be so for me? And what about this model for my friendships with women informs me as a feminist therapist? To answer these questions I have found useful the notion of the "wounded healer," the therapist who is able to offer healing in large part because of her own experience of being wounded emotionally and healing from those wounds. I think in particular of my on-line "grrlfriends" as we style ourselves (a word derived from the Riot Grrl movement, which reclaimed the term "girl" as a ferocious, powerful word to describe a woman). This relationship has, more than any other, helped me to heal the wounds of being the outsider girl. So I must ask, what has it taught me that informs me more particularly in my work as a feminist therapist than do other of my experiences of healing the wounds of earlier attempts at friendships with women?

One of the factors that I have realized is absent from our daily exchanges is that of shame or humiliation. These painful affects are core components of relational wounding, experienced subjectively as traumatic by many persons who have had such difficult encounters. Each of us in our trio has written to the other two of her most potentially shame-inducing thoughts, feelings, and actions over the years; we know one another's faithless thoughts, petty angers, moments of cowardice in addition to our hopes and fears and joys. And to each of these disclosures the other two have responded with love and compassion. The fact that we have made our mutual confessions to our screens and keyboards is, I believe, an important component of how we have learned to take these risks with one another. We have simultaneously both intense intimacy and utter privacy.

I can imagine that each and both of my grrlfriends has read some of my emails with a sinking heart, or with feelings of exasperation or disapproval. But I have not had to face those difficult responses in person, and they have been completely filtered through the time it has taken to read my emails, compose (and perhaps delete the first two or three versions of) a response. I've never asked either of them about this; I simply know that the emotional high-wire acts that I have engaged in with them were made possible for me in part by the distance inherent in our mode of connection. This may not be true for either one of them; it is certainly the case for me.

As a feminist therapist I have come to see the parallels in clients' lives of the effects of shame on the willingness to risk in the relational context of psychotherapy, and the importance of emotional privacy even in the context of intimacy and disclosure. Transparency should not be the equivalent of being forcibly exposed; many of the survivors of complex trauma with whom I have worked come to therapy with no ability to differentiate between these two constructs. I consequently do whatever I can in my role as a therapist to reduce shame for my clients, including making it possible for some of them to use email themselves as a means of conveying the information and emotions that feel too tender to deliver in person.

I am likely more open to the use of electronic communication with my clients than are many other psychotherapists of my age cohort because of my experience with my grrlfriends. I know from 16 years of intense yet utterly private closeness with these two dear women that for some wounded humans, particularly those whose traumas have been primarily relational in nature, the safety of screen and keyboard allow for possibilities of transparency and vulnerability that are terrifying and near-impossible with the other human in the room.

As a feminist therapist with a primary interest in empowering the people with whom I work, I have learned that making such a venue for communication available to some people empowers them. Rather than shoehorning the many survivors of complex trauma with whom I work into the requirement that disclosure must occur in the context that most frightens—and thus disempowers—them, the presence of another human being who is more powerful than they are relationally, I have parlayed the many strands of my narrative of friendships with women into a willingness to think creatively about how to co-construct safe spaces for our work. I think of it as an interesting recipe; take one part knowing what it feels like to be shamed and on the outside, one part knowing the power of emotional intimacy and support, blend carefully with the private-not-private space of email. Yield—one deepened appreciation for the healing power of connection, and an equally profound respect for the necessity of control over how those connections are titrated.

CONCLUSION

I often listen to music while writing; today's work was accompanied by the Dixie Chicks' rousing song of female friendship, "Goodbye Earl." In this song, Mary Anne comes back home from her exciting life outside the small town of her childhood to rescue her best friend Wanda from her abusive husband, Earl, who has put her into intensive care with his latest beating. Mary Ann literally kills for her best friend. It's a tad disconcerting for this feminist non-violence advocate to listen to the lyrics cheerfully celebrating the poisoning of Earl and the happy picnic accompanying dumping his remains in the local lake. It's not what I would do, or want a friend to do for me. But it's a sentiment that I can absolutely recognize today; my women friends are the people for whom I would do anything, go anywhere, take risks if that's what they needed from me, and they would do, and have done that for me.

My friends have raised my standards about what is possible and expectable in relationships between humans. In that regard, that have made me a wiser and better therapist, one who can hold out that standard and the hope for its achievement in the work I do with my clients. Feminist therapy and friendship are strands of my life story that are inextricably intertwined.

REFERENCES

Brown, L. S. (1994). *Subversive dialogues: Theory in feminist therapy.* New York: Basic Books.

Brown, L. S. (2009). *Feminist therapy.* Washington, DC: American Psychological Association.

Chesler, P. (1972). *Women and madness.* Garden City, NY: Doubleday.

Crick, N. R. & Rose, A. J. (2000). Toward a gender-balanced approach to the study of social-emotional development: A look at relational aggression. In Patricia H. Miller & Ellin Kofsky Scholnick (Eds.), *Toward a feminist developmental psychology* (pp. 153–168). Florence, KY: Taylor & Frances.

Hadley, M. R. (2003). Relational, indirect, adaptive, or just mean: Recent work on aggression in adolescent girls – Part I. *Studies in gender and sexuality, 4,* 367–394.

Lamb, S. (2002). *The secret lives of girls: What good girls really do.* New York: Simon and Schuster.

Weisstein, N. (1968). *Kinder, kuche, kirche as scientific law: Psychology constructs the female.* Boston: New England Free Press.

Acts of Remembering: Relationship in Feminist Therapy

SHERRI TAYLOR

The Wright Institute, Berkeley, California

This article is an act of remembering. In the first part of this article, the author remembers and reflects upon her own journey of being and becoming a feminist, healer and clinical psychologist in training. She then shares some of the most meaningful lessons on 1) the therapeutic alliance, 2) transference and countertransference, 3) the nature of change, and 4) cultural competence that she has learned from her sister of the heart relationship with the brilliant spirit and work of Black lesbian, feminist, warrior poet, and activist, Audre Lorde. In each of these lessons the author reflects on her efforts to translate her conceptual or applied practice as a feminist student therapist. It is her hope to invite exploration of new bridges and paths by which other feminist psychologists may connect more deeply and meaningfully to our work both professionally and personally. The author closes with some reflections on the path ahead for feminist psychology.

INTRODUCTION

I was not part of the sweat and fire that birthed a woman of color politics in this country in the 1970s and the 1980s. This is why I want to remember that I have been shaped by it. It is why I am indebted to the women who literally entered the fire for me, on my behalf.

– M. Jacqui Alexander, *Pedagogies of crossing*, p. 260

When I received the invitation to write on the subject of female friendships, feminism, and psychotherapy I was thrilled. When I sat down to actually begin writing I had no idea how to begin. How would I narrow my focus? About which aspect of women's influence in my life would I write? For as long as I can remember women's culture, women's narratives, and women's friendships have served as a critical landscape against and within which my life has unfolded. I grew up in a relatively small, working class and predominately Black community in Dallas, Texas. My childhood was filled with church ladies, Big Mamas, Madeas, and Sista So-and-Sos. Many of my fondest memories are of times spent with my Grandmama, an amazing woman who offered healing through food, laughter, and hard love. The powerful influence of women in Southern culture and particularly in Black Southern culture has always been an important and comforting piece of my experience. I'm not referring to a mythologized culture of the Black Matriarch, but of the primacy of Black women's roles as keepers of spirit in family and community. From a very young age I understood the value and importance of female friendships. It wasn't until I was introduced to one of the women who "entered the fire for me" that I saw all of us, including myself, as singular yet integral points connected in an ancient and infinite lineage of brave and fearless women of color.

As the quote that began this article says, although I was not a part of that movement, I am a direct descendant of that lineage. This article is an act of remembering. However, remembering can be a tricky thing. M. Jacqui Alexander (2005) notes, "Remembering is different from looking back. We can look back sideways and not bring things into full view" (p. 275). In the first part of this article, I am remembering my own journey of being and becoming a feminist, healer and clinical psychologist in training. I will then share some of the most meaningful lessons I have learned from the brilliant spirit and work of Black lesbian, feminist, warrior poet, and activist, Audre Lorde. In sharing these lessons and reflecting on my efforts to translate them into my practice as a feminist student therapist, I hope to offer a new bridges and paths by which other feminist psychologists may connect more deeply and meaningfully to the work both professionally and personally. Finally, I will close with some reflections on the path ahead for feminist psychology.

FEMINIST BEGINNINGS

It was the summer of 1993, and I was between my freshman and sophomore years at Stanford University. My best friend and I had taken a summer job in North Lake Tahoe that we envisioned would give us the kinds of experiences worthy of a blockbuster coming of age movie. Well, we were very wrong. Our very long days consisted of monotonous manual labor and very little leisure time. Needless to say that summer did not provide any of the freewheeling shenanigans my nearly nineteen year-old mind had envisioned during my first summer away from home and the eyes and ears of my Mama and Daddy.

Desperate for some measure of excitement, every night after work we would drive to a local 24-hour hotel café, drink coffee and pretend we were adults. We made grand plans and prepared for the jet-setting lives of fortune and fame we incorrectly assumed our highly priced college educations would guarantee. Because we fancied ourselves to be sophisticated intellectual types and because we were bored as you-know-what we decided to start our own book club. Having packed for activities less sedentary than reading, we went to the local bookstore to find our first selection. After a few hours, we decided on *The Women's Room* by Marilyn French, a meaty paperback with a muddy olive green cover. The title was imprinted with a simple black font and showed the words "The Ladies' Room" with "Ladies" crossed out and "Women's" written over it in a bright pink graffiti-style font. (I think we might have chosen it simply because there were two copies!) I had no idea that for $6.95 my life was about to change in fundamental and irreversible ways. For the next two months I voraciously read any and everything related to feminism and the women's movement that I could get my hands on. Shulamith Firestone. Simone de Beauvior. Catherine MacKinnon. Combahee River Collective. Patricia Hill Collins. bell hooks. Gloria Anzaldúa. Angela Y. Davis. Cherríe Moraga. Adrienne Rich. I was hooked on this thing called feminism.

Inspired by the consciousness raising groups mentioned in our summer reading, when we returned from our summer of transformation we began to host "consciousness-lowering" gatherings or as we called them, CL groups. We called them consciousness-lowering groups because we were trying to lower our inhibitions as a group of over-achieving Stanford students—and we often had wine with our meals. We had a steady core group of five to six women who got together once a month and talked about the issues we felt were important to us as young women from diverse sociocultural backgrounds trying to thrive in the university setting. Amazing things began to happen. We had literary themed CL groups and read the poetry of women like Margaret Atwood, Merle Woo, Gwendolyn Brooks, and Lucille Clifton. We shared food and secrets. We explored women's music and through the songs of the Indigo Girls, Sweet Honey in the Rock, Joni Mitchell, Ani di Franco, Joan Armatrading, Tracy Chapman, and Tori Amos. We introduced ourselves to a bridge built by the writings of radical women of color (Moraga, C., and Anzaldúa, G., 1983). We were afraid and we were brave. We cried and fought and laughed and cried again. Our final gathering for the year featured a kiddie pool and my coming out as a woman who loved women. What I remember most was that we loved each other fiercely.

It was 1994. *Forrest Gump* topped the box-office, the world lost Kurt Cobain and Jackie O., the North American Free Trade Agreement began, the Wonderbra was "invented," and a first-class stamp cost 29 cents.

Concurrent to the feminist education I was getting from monthly CL groups, I was also taking Feminist Studies coursework and declared Feminist Studies as my major soon thereafter. The program's interdisciplinary design allowed me to take classes across multiple disciplines including cultural anthropology, art history, political science, history, linguistics, and religious studies. Any area of scholarly inquiry was available to me. Feminism's critical perspectives gave me a language and framework to examine power and oppression as they are woven into discourses of race, ethnicity, class, sexuality, ability, and gender. I was also validated in my deep appreciation for embodied experience, and encouraged to think critically about the production and uses of knowledge and power. I graduated with a degree in Feminist Studies with an emphasis in culture, media, and representational practices.

Given the pressures of student loans and a thing called rent, like many liberal arts majors, after graduation I stumbled into a career in marketing. I never stopped looking for a way to create a life of service to others that drew upon my academic background as well as my life experiences. In my first attempt at this I decided to enter a master's program in Women's Studies at a state university with every intention to become a professor of Women's Studies. (I was also working a 40-plus-hour a week job.) I remember one particularly long and lonely bus ride home when I began to question whether I was on a track or a path—and more importantly, which was the one for me. I was researching and writing about the effects of institutional oppression and the path to liberation and empowerment on a purely theoretical level, however what I longed to do was actively bring these theories into practical application through direct service. I realized I was not doing the work that I was passionate about.

I have always known that my calling was, in the broadest sense, to be a healer. Many of the women in my family possessed gifts of healing. I grew up with a mother who performed faith healings, danced in ecstatic joy when she was filled with the Holy Spirit, and used her prophetic visions and dreams to help others. She always told me I was a healer. I searched for a profession that would allow me to integrate my feminist practices, cultural values, and belief in social justice with my desire to facilitate healing at the individual and systemic levels. It was time for me to take my experiences and forge a new path. At the age of 35 I left my job and returned to school as a full-time graduate student in a clinical psychology doctoral program. Every day I am grateful for that decision.

My life and work is deeply informed by my feminist beginnings and draws upon a diverse range of disciplines, theories, and sources of knowledge that include and extend beyond the borders of psychology. In addition to the psychological research and theories that shape my research, you will find feminist theorists, cultural theorists, sociologists, historians, poets, spiritual traditions and the deep cultural and embodied wisdom of the strong, resilient Black and Native American women and men who are my ancestors. I know that my sociocultural and political locations as a queer feminist woman of color contribute significantly to what I understand to the purpose of my clinical work, what kind of research interests me, and how I make sense of my experiences in the academy. For me, the personal is the political is the professional.

LEARNING HOW TO SURVIVE IN THE MASTER'S HOUSE

I was introduced to Black Feminist Thought, Womanist Theory and the world of feminist women of color through the work of Audre Lorde. I remember reading the poem "A Litany for Survival" (Lorde, 1978, p. 31-32) and having what I can only understand as a spiritual experience. Since our first introduction many years ago I can say with confidence that Audre has become one of my fiercest and most ardent sisters of the heart. Audre's inimitable voice continues to draw me towards a deeper understanding of the standards to which I must hold myself accountable in the context of relationship. She also stands sentinel against those forces of oppression that seek to leave me disillusioned and unfocused. She nurtures a critical understanding of many of my personal experiences as a queer Black feminist pursuing a doctoral degree.

In September of 1979 Audre Lorde delivered a speech at the last panel on the last day of the Second Sex Conference in New York. Invited at "the last hour" to participate in what was the only panel "where the input of Black feminists and lesbians [was] represented," she used the occasion to direct attention to not only the heteropatriarcal underpinnings, but also the classist and colonialist discourses inherent in the practices that structured the conference (Lorde, 1984d, p. 110). Audre asked, "What does it mean when the tools of a racist patriarchy are used to examine the fruits of that same patriarchy?" (Lorde, 1984d, pp. 110–111). That speech, "The master's tools will never dismantle the master's house," is now a staple of contemporary feminist theory and one that I refer to often.

On my travels as a woman of color through the master's house of the academy she has inspired me, encouraged me and guided me while at the same time gently and firmly reminding me that,

> Those of us who stand outside the circle of this society's definition of acceptable women; those of us who have been forged in the crucibles of difference—those of us who are poor, who are lesbians, who are Black, who are older—know that *survival is not an academic skill.* It is learning how to stand alone, unpopular and sometimes reviled, and how to make common cause with those others identified as outside structures in order to define a world in which we can all flourish. (Lorde, 1984d, p. 112, emphasis in original)

Her book *Sister Outsider* sits in my bookcase lodged neatly between the *Diagnostic and Statistical Manual of Mental Disorders, Fourth Edition—Text Revision* (DSM-IV-TR) and Etiony Aldarondo's *Advancing Social Justice Though Clinical Practice.*

Audre has been a constant reminder that in many ways my scholarly and professional education is also teaching me a language and set of practices rooted in ideologies and discourses that used to heal and to oppress. How will I use them? In an interview with her own sister of the heart Adrienne Rich, Audre comments that the learning and practice of rational science "is not unnecessary. ... It serves to get from this place to that place. But if you don't honor those places, then the road is meaningless." (Lorde, 1984c, p. 100). This is something I must not forget. This article is an act of remembering.

In the spirit of remembering I want to briefly share a few of the lessons she has offered to me, how I have tried to translate them into my clinical work and how they have facilitated deeper and more meaningful connections to my work with clients, my profession, and myself.

Lesson #1: The Therapeutic Alliance

> Poetry is the way we help give name to the nameless so it can be thought.... As they become known to and accepted by us, our feelings and the honest exploration of them become sanctuaries and spawning grounds for the most radical and daring ideas.
>
> – Lorde, 1984d, p. 37

Audre has taught me that a critical part of becoming a healer is learning to bear witness to the chaos of people's lives so that they might find a way into the poetry of their experience. The poetry Audre refers to is not "the sterile word play" taught to us, but "a revelatory distillation of experience" that "lays the foundations for a future of change" (Lorde, 1984d, pp. 37–38). Using this technique in my practice of feminist therapy has showed me that connecting individuals to the poetry of their experience while witnessing the painful and sometimes unjust realities of their suffering is an important first step toward healing complex historical, structural, and experiential traumas. It introduces the possibility for narratives of oppression to be transformed by moments of resistance and resilience.

In the summer of 2011, I worked at an Oakland organization with a group of predominantly African-American and Latino young men and women under the supervision of the juvenile justice system. I remember one young man in particular. His father had been incarcerated for the majority of his young life. His brother had been murdered earlier that year. He told me it didn't matter much to him that he wasn't in juvenile hall because he was still locked up in his head.

In our final therapy session he sat draped across his usual chair—his nearly six-foot frame cradled awkwardly like a child in the sturdy arms of an adult. Like many youth I have worked with from under-resourced communities and multiply stressed families, he often struggled to imagine his own future so I asked him to imagine what he thought I wished most for him. He inhaled deeply as his eyes rose slowly to the ceiling welling up with tears. He smiled and exhaled the word "freedom." All the air suddenly left the room. Something sacred and otherworldly had come to join us. Together we sat in silence. I still have no words to describe what that moment felt like; I am only reminded of an old saying that a poem is never complete until somebody hears it.

Lesson # 2: Transference and Countertransference

> Our erotic knowledge empowers us, becomes a lens through which we scrutinize all aspects of our existence, forcing us to evaluate those aspects of our existence honestly in terms of their relative meaning within our lives.
>
> – Lorde, 1984 g, p. 57

Highlighting the profound value and importance of embodied experience Audre defines the erotic as "a measure against the beginnings of our sense of self and the chaos of our strongest feelings." (Lorde, 1984g, p. 54). According to Audre European-American traditions teach us to fear and turn away from our erotic knowledge, which she believes often results in the misnaming or misrecognition of what is different and what is shared. She writes, "the need for sharing deep feeling is a human need" (Lorde, 1984g, p. 58).

Feminist theory has taught me that particularly for women and those who are oppressed reconnecting to the embodied experience is crucial to psychological healing. My desire to understand how to apply my theoretical knowledge of embodiment as a means to resist oppression in the service of healing has led me to study somatic and body-centered approaches like sensorimotor and focusing psychotherapy approaches (Ogden, Minton, and Pain, 2006; Gendlin, 1982; Rappaport, 2009). I have noticed that when I am fearless and allow my embodied knowledge to supplement and inform my therapeutic interventions I find it is often easier to facilitate a clients' (re) connection to their own embodied experience—the effects of which can be profound.

As a part of my clinical education each year I am placed at a practicum site to receive supervised training. This past year I have been working at a community mental health clinic serving people with co-occuring disorders. Sometime ago I was working with an African-American female client who came to me in crisis. Although she had been in recovery from alcohol and substance use for over ten years, her sociocultural context and ethnic minority heritage located her on the downside of power in multiple areas of her lived experience. During our sessions she often oscillated between a rigid and immobilized or a collapsed and closed body posture. On this day she sat in the chair across from me like a piece of crumpled paper, her head cradled in her hand and eyes downcast. She was physically and psychologically bent over by her distress. She often talked about feeling stuck. I noticed her hands trembled in her lap and when she spoke the tension in her jaw seemed to limit the full mobility of her mouth. When we began the session I gave myself permission to use my embodied experience of sitting with her to guide my intervention. Often the body tells a story that words cannot. As I sank deeply into our shared experience, I had an overwhelming desire to break free from something. I wanted to run.

Based on this embodied knowledge I suggested that we stand up together. Initially she seemed confused and I encouraged her to simply entertain the idea and then tell me what it felt like. She agreed and we stood up. Our session turned the proverbial corner. She immediately noticed and located a sensation near her stomach that she described as warm. I shared with her that in some cultures the area of the body she referred to was associated with a sense or personal power. I encouraged her to move her body around in any way that felt right. As she began to walk around the small room her voice grew stronger and she shared the depth and intensity of her desire for a better relationship with her children and her father. Embodied knowledge exists in a deep place of spirit, memory, and desire, and it produces the type of clarity and insight that willfully speaks truth to power.

Lesson # 3: The Nature of Change

> And yes, it is very difficult to stand still and to listen to another woman's voice delineate an agony I do not share, or one to which I myself have contributed.
>
> – Lorde, 1984f, p. 128

Audre challenges me not only to accompany my clients as they examine the texture and intricate details of their experience, but also to not be naïve to the likelihood that my privilege is underwritten by another's oppression. She asks, "What woman's terms of oppression have become precious and necessary to her as a ticket into the fold of righteous away from the cold winds of self-scrutiny?" (Lorde, 1984f, p. 132). I must resist and critically examine any impulse that I might have to ignore or distort another's anger toward their oppression in order to spare my own feelings of guilt. Audre writes, "guilt ... becomes a device to protect ignorance and the continuation of things the way they are, the ultimate protection for changelessness" (Lorde, 1984f, p. 130).

In the therapeutic context I am learning to be open to the possibility that change is initiated not only for my client but also for me, the clinician.

Audre refers to a type of change that is "not a simple switch of positions or a temporary lessening of tensions, not the ability to smile or feel good" but rather "a basic and radical alteration in those assumptions underlining our lives" (Lorde, 1984f, p. 127). Audre firmly reminds me "I am not free while any [person] is unfree, even when [their] shackles are very different from my own" (Lorde, 1984f, pp. 132–133). Do I listen for critical connections to broader and more densely woven discourses of power and oppression in a client's expression of anger or do I only hear symptoms or "pathology"? Can I make room to hear both? The dynamic process of change that occurs *in* relationship asks for a response. And what will I do with the knowledge that I might hold a key to another's shackles? How will *I* change?

Lesson #4: Cultural Competence

> But we have no patterns for relating across our human differences as equals. As a result, those differences have been misnamed and misused in the service of separation and confusion. ... But it is not those differences between us that are separating us. It is rather our refusal to recognize those differences, and to examine the distortions which result from our misnaming them and their effects upon human behavior and expectation.
>
> — Lorde, 1984a, p. 115

In this act of remembering Audre's work, I have noticed strong critiques of practices of ignorance are a common theme linking many of her public speeches and non-fiction prose. As a discipline psychology has put great effort and resources toward refining its techniques of knowledge production, however Audre might suggest that equal attention be given to understanding and identifying the processes and practices used to manage, structure and institutionalize the perpetuation of ignorance as knowledge.

As recently as 2006 a survey of professional psychologists found that overall participants did not "practice what they preached" with regard to culturally competent therapy (Hansen et.al., 2006). This practice of ignorance concerns me greatly for as Sullivan and Tuana have written "practices of ignorance are often intertwined with practices of oppression and exclusion" (Sullivan and Tuana, 2007, p. 9). The ignorance, dismissal or misrecognition of difference has direct implications for clinical practice, and psychologists have the capacity and obligation to intervene in this process. How do I continue to initiate critical examination of those professional practices that manage, structure, and institutionalize the production of ignorance?

Audre suggests that I develop the clinical skills and reflective practices that allow me to recognize difference *and* examine the possible distortions that result from misnaming them (Lorde, 1984a, p. 122). The recognition to which Audre refers is not a tokenizing or uncritical recognition of difference as deviance, but rather a deep and sometimes painful acknowledgement of how our very lives are often built upon the misrecognition of difference so that it is easier to turn away from it. Does my understanding of difference incorporate resistance, resilience, conflict and struggle? Do I misrecognize difference as deviance to mask histories of oppression?

As feminists who are psychologists Audre exhorts us to be relentless in our examination of those practices of knowledge production that are complicit in the production of ignorance. According to Cheryl Townsend Gilkes, "[feminists] must recognize the difference between the master's house and the master's illicit occupation of a house that should not be the master's to control. The racist and sexist imaginations have squatted in the spaces of cultural definition for too long." (Fiorenza, Brown, Gilkes, Hunt, and Barstow, 1985, p. 82). To engage with these distortions encourages a focus that extends beyond considering the intersecting identities of *other* people to one that is based on an analysis of difference that attends to power, interconnectedness, and what Chandra Mohanty has called "mutuality and coimplication" (Mohanty, 2003b, p. 242). Specifically coimplication refers to the recognition of difference as a shared process that is part of larger geopolitical and sociocultural systems (Mohanty, 2003a, p. 203).

A feminist therapy approach that actively incorporates coimplication invites the therapist to take an orientation of solidarity and include a simultaneous focus on the individual and collective experiences of power, privilege, oppression, and resistance. It's not a comfortable edge. Attempting to work from a place of coimplication is in many ways similar to engaging in what Bernice Johnson Reagon called coalition work. Coimplication like coalition work is uncomfortable, attends to multiple issues simultaneously, and is something you must practice "everyday you get up and find yourself alive" (Reagon, B., 1983, p. 368). That we live in the master's house is not the problem, but we ought to be aware of *how* we pay rent, *who* is signing the checks, and *from whose* account the funds are drawn because "it is difficult to remember that the war against dehumanization is ceaseless" (Lorde, 1984a, p. 119). There are no easy answers and I must be committed to wrestling with these issues personally and professionally.

LIGHT AND PROGRESS – REMEMBERING OUR VISION

> And to acknowledge our dreams is to sometimes acknowledge the distance between those dreams and our present situation. Acknowledged, our dreams can shape the realities of our future if we arm them with the hard work and scrutiny of now.
>
> — Lorde, 1984b, p.153

I find it somehow appropriate that I am writing my final reflections about relationships, lineage, and connection to women as I sit at the kitchen table in Dallas, Texas where my first and most primary female relationship was forged. I am watching my Mama shuffle around the kitchen in her familiar way. She is softly singing gospel music as she moves about the house. Something about this moment feels so complete.

Love inspires remembering (Alexander, 2005, p. 279). This article is an act of remembering. Feminist psychology must sustain and remember our connection to the movements, relationships and experiences which birthed our practices and nurtures our ever developing critical consciousness. By remembering the vision and emancipatory projects of feminism not as a memorial, but as a living text from which we might learn anew, we can examine how we have misread or misrecognized differences between and among ourselves—and those with whom we work. Through these practices of remembrance, we grant ourselves and the practice and profession of psychology the possibility of empowering and socially just practices of knowing and we keep alive the creative stuff that drives us to do this work.

Ultimately, I believe my feminist beginnings and sister of the heart relationship with Audre has had a significant impact on my relationship to *being in relationship*. I am learning that I am more capable of creating the best possible conditions for healing when I allow the multiple currents of my spiritual, professional, and inherited lineages to be present and actively in relationship. As I allow these sources of knowledge and living to flow through me in the service of healing, I am reminded of a final lesson that my sister of the heart relationship with Audre has taught me:

> Every woman I have ever loved has left her print upon me, where I loved some invaluable piece of myself apart from me—so different that I had to stretch and grow in order to recognize her. And in that growing, we came to ... that place where work begins. (Lorde, 1982, p. 255)

REFERENCES

Aldarondo, E. (Ed.) (2007). *Advancing social justice through clinical practice.* Hillsdale, NJ: Lawrence Erlbaum Associates.

Alexander, M. J. (2005). Remembering *This Bridge Called My Back*, remembering ourselves. In *Pedagogies of crossing.* Durham, NC: Duke University Press.

Gendlin, E. T. (1982). *Focusing.* (2nd ed.). New York: Bantam Books.

Fiorenza, E. S., Brown, K. M., Gilkes, C. T., Hunt, M. E., & Barstow, A. L. (1985). Roundtable discussion: On feminist methodology. *Journal of Feminist Studies in Religion, 1*(2), 73–88.

Hansen, N. D., Randazzo, K. V., Schwartz, A., Marshall, M., Kalis, D., Frazier, R., ... Norvig, G. (2006). Do we practice what we preach? An exploratory survey of multicultural psychotherapy competencies. *Professional Psychology: Research and Practice, 37*(1), 66–74. doi: 10.1037/0735-7028.37.1.66

Lorde, A. (1978). A litany for survival. In *The black unicorn* (pp. 31–32). New York: W. W. Norton & Company, Inc.

Lorde, A. (1984a). Age, race, class, and sex: Women redefining difference. In *Sister outsider* (pp. 114–123). Freedom, CA: The Crossing Press.

Lorde, A. (1984b). Eye to eye: Black women, hatred, and anger. In *Sister outsider* (pp. 145–175). Freedom, CA: The Crossing Press.

Lorde, A. (1984c). An interview: Audre Lorde and Adrienne Rich. In *Sister outsider* (pp. 81–109). Freedom, CA: The Crossing Press.

Lorde, A. (1984d). Poetry is not a luxury. In *Sister outsider* (pp. 36–9). Freedom, CA: The Crossing Press.

Lorde, A. (1984e). The master's tools will never dismantle the master's house. In *Sister outsider* (pp. 110–113). Freedom, CA: The Crossing Press.

Lorde, A. (1984f). The uses of anger: Women responding to racism. In *Sister outsider* (pp. 124–133). Freedom, CA: The Crossing Press.

Lorde, A. (1984g). Uses of the erotic: The erotic as power. In *Sister outsider* (pp. 53–59). Freedom, CA: The Crossing Press.

Lorde, A. (1982). *Zami: A new spelling of my name.* Freedom, CA: The Crossing Press.

Mohanty, C. T. (2003a). Race, multiculturalism, and pedagogies of dissent. In *Feminism without borders: Decolonizing theory, practicing solidarity* (p. 190–217). Durham, NC: Duke University Press.

Mohanty, C.T. (2003b). "Under western eyes" revisited: Feminist solidarity through anticapitalist struggles. In *Feminism without orders: Decolonizing theory, practicing solidarity* (pp. 221–251). Durham, NC: Duke University Press.

Moraga, C., & Anzaldúa, G. (1983). This *Bridge Called My Back*: Writings By Radical Women of Color. New York: Kitchen Table Press.

Ogden, P., Minton, P., & Pain, C. (2006). *Trauma and the Body: A sensorimotor approach to psychotherapy.* New York: W. W. Norton & Company.

Rappaport, L. (2009). *Focusing-oriented art therapy: Accessing the body's wisdom and creative intelligence.* Philadelphia, PA: Jessica Kingsley.

Reagon, B. J. (1983). Coalition Politics: Turning the Century. In B. Smith (Ed.) *Home girls: A Black feminist anthology* (pp. 356–368). New York: Kitchen Table.

Sullivan, S., & Tuana, N. (2007). *Race and epistemologies of ignorance.* Albany, NY: State University of New York Press.

Growing at the Hyphen: Female Friendships and Social Context

PRATYUSHA TUMMALA-NARRA
Boston College, Boston, Massachusetts

Although the psychological literature has focused more on immigrant women's roles in their families, women's friendships are important sources of support and identity development. This article explores the development of friendship in the context of immigration, cultural adaptation, becoming a template for identity and intimacy. Specifically, the author describes a personal friendship and a psychotherapy case vignette, integrating feminist, multicultural, and relational psychoanalytic perspectives, to illustrate the influence of female friendship in coping with loss, acculturative stress, discrimination, and the formation of bicultural identity. These examples highlight the ways in which personal friendships of the therapist and the client contribute to the psychotherapeutic relationship, growth in intimacy and authenticity, and the negotiation of a hyphenated identity.

Throughout the 20th century in American society, women's relationships with men, particularly heterosexual relationships, dominated mainstream cultural images of women and the feminine. The rise of feminism in the 1960s and 1970s challenged images of friendships between women as centered on superficiality and competition for male attention (Castaneda & Burns-Glover, 2008). Women's friendships have more recently been considered as primary sources for support and identity development. In fact, there is ample evidence indicating the positive impact of positive female friendships on women's physical and psychological well-being (Knickmeyer,

Sexton, & Nishimura, 2002). Although a core part of female experience, the nature of women's friendships and the contexts within which they develop have been largely overlooked in the psychological literature. In particular, immigrant women's friendships have received little attention, at least in part due to our discipline's interest in their roles within their families rather than their social networks (Mand, 2006).

Various social changes and stressors have been implicated in the transformation of women's friendships more broadly in contemporary society, such as geographic mobility and demands of working inside and outside the home (Castaneda & Burns-Glover, 2008; Miller & Stiver, 1997). O'Connor (1992) has suggested that friendships are constructed within and reflect social and cultural ideologies and realities. This article considers how friendship grows in the midst of cultural adaptation, and becomes a primary template for the development of identity and intimacy. Little (1989) described distinctions between social friends, those with whom we share common interests, familiar friends with whom we recreate relationships from early in life, and communicating friends, those who generate transformative change. Although a rare friendship holds all of these different possibilities (Akhtar, 2011), the one I will share in this article reflects such a combination. I describe this friendship in the context of immigration and social change, and how this bond has transformed my personal identity and my work as a psychotherapist who integrates feminist, multicultural, and psychodynamic orientations. A clinical case vignette will further illustrate the role of friendship, intimacy and the context of immigration in psychotherapy with women.

MEETING AT THE HYPHEN

I was born in Hyderabad, India, and Ami was born in Flint, Michigan. Her family speaks Gujarati and mine speaks Telugu. Ami and I met when we were 14 years old at a Hindu temple in Flint. She approached me at a function, and asked from where I had moved. I had recently moved to Michigan with my family, after living in the East Coast (New York City and an all-White community in New Jersey) for seven years. Since leaving India at age 7, I hadn't experienced a sense of home until we moved to Michigan. My life in New Jersey often felt lonely. This was the era of the Dot Busters, street gangs in New Jersey, who physically assaulted and killed people of South Asian descent. The "dot" in "Dot Busters" referred to the "bindi," a Hindu religious symbol, worn by Hindu women. Many of my memories of living in New Jersey at that time involved experiences of overt racism, such as when our home was vandalized and my older brother and I were targets of verbal assaults and physical threats.

Soon after arriving in Michigan, my parents enrolled me in a Hindu youth class that met every Sunday. There were only about ten students in the class, all teenagers living on the hyphen, either born in the U.S. or emigrated from India to the U.S. as young children. This was the first time since living in India that I had regular interactions with a group of Indian peers. I remembered feeling relieved but not realizing at the time the reasons behind my renewed sense of comfort. Ami, being born and raised in Flint, knew the landscape of this Indian community. While I felt somewhat anxious in my new surroundings, Ami appeared confident and comfortable with herself. In retrospect, I had hoped to feel as real and confident as Ami seemed to me. Knowing what I have come to know about her over the past 28 years, I imagine that she either consciously or unconsciously could see my anxiety and my wish to belong, and responded by taking care of me.

As in the case of many immigrant origin women, my friendship with Ami began as a function of our interactions within the Indian American community. Social networks for immigrants and their children are often located within their ethnic and/or religious communities. Akhtar (2011) has written about the importance of homoethnic friends in the immigrant's adjustment to the new country. He highlighted the ways in which shared cultural experiences such as historical points of reference, food preferences, cultural and religious festivals, provide the basis for close bonds and "emotional refueling." This refueling is essential as immigrants mourn for loss of familiarity and connection with people and places left behind in the country of origin. Further, there often develops a sense of kinship, belonging, and "instantaneous mutual recognition" (Akhtar, 2011, p. 86). For first generation, this recognition is evident in collective memories of the country of origin. This mutual recognition is also important to the second generation, and manifests in the shared hyphenated quality of cultural experience and belonging. In fact, the term "ABCD" or "American-born confused desi," recognized among Asian Indians in the U.S., is used to describe the shifting nature of cultural identity experienced by second generation Asian Indians.

Sirin and Fine (2007) suggested that hyphenated identities are "at once joined, and separated, by history, the present, socio-political climate, geography, biography, longings, and loss" (p. 152). The hyphen for immigrants reflects the transformation of relationships with family and friends as influenced by the social context. Since our adolescence, Ami and I have been partners in both defying and embracing the hyphen. We grew up with similar cultural values and norms that guided our interactions with family and community. We each had an older brother, and were the only daughter in each of our families. As adolescents, we struggled on the hyphen with our strong identifications with close family ties and our growing curiosity about life outside our families. As in the case of girls in other immigrant communities (Suarez-Orozco & Qin, 2006), we were monitored more closely and faced more restrictions in socializing with friends when compared with our brothers and other Indian boys. This monitoring by our parents, "aunties" and "uncles" in the community at times felt caring and protective, and other times felt unfair and stifling. To complicate things, there were few available models for how to approach these conflicts. Some of our peers coped with these conflicts through "counterphobic assimilation," by separating from the Indian community and interacting only with mainstream culture (Akhtar, 2011). Others identified strongly with their parents' fears of losing cultural identity and interacted only within the Indian community. The stress accompanying the negotiation of this "bicultural tightrope" (Roland, 2006) contributed to feelings of loneliness and isolation. It felt impossible to talk with our parents about these experiences as we were well aware of their own struggles with acculturation. Friendship became essential to survival on the hyphen.

BICULTURAL IDENTIFICATIONS

The bicultural anxiety that characterized much of my adolescence and early adulthood contributed to a split in my Indian identity and my emerging American identity. The chasm between these two sets of identification grew wider in my college years. Socializing with my Indian American peers helped me to develop socially, despite restrictions on typical mainstream adolescent socializing, such as dating and going out with friends in the evening hours. At the same time, I was increasingly interested in making friends from different cultural backgrounds, and became more active on my college campus. While I moved away to college to a different city in Michigan, Ami lived at home and commuted to her college. We had spent two years of our adolescence spending much of our social time together with our female friends in the Indian community, laughing and crying over what we both liked and disliked about our Indian background, talking about our lives at school, and making plans for shopping and watching movies. During our college years, we spent most of our time separately, developing friendships outside of the Indian community. Yet, the friendships I had formed in my adolescence created a sense of home for which I had longed since leaving India.

Although Ami and I did not talk as frequently over the next several years, I had always experienced her as a sister who I could turn to when I most needed one. Interestingly, we independently developed interests in pursuing careers that involved healing. Ami studied physical therapy and I studied psychology. In retrospect, this is not surprising as the experience of growth and change has felt important to both us throughout our lives. Our friendship deepened in graduate school, when she and I lived together for a summer when she had completed a clinical rotation in the same city where I had been working on my doctoral studies. In some ways, we kept our unguarded style of related from our adolescence, but we began to integrate what we had come to learn about ourselves in college, and looked to the future. We were absorbed in our academic and career goals, and in sorting out romantic relationships. We supported each other through disappointment with relationships, and through mounting pressure from our parents to get married. We asked ourselves and each other what it would mean to marry someone Indian or non-Indian. While we strongly identified with our parents' wishes for us to marry someone with a similar cultural background, we once again found ourselves questioning their position. We wondered if we would lose our Indian identity if we married someone who is not Indian, and whether we would be expected to be traditional spouses like our mothers whose personal desires and ambitions were secondary to that of our fathers. We also talked about how our experiences of spirituality shifted since adolescence, and questioned the role of women in religious institutions. We had each tried to find more personal meaning in our spiritual practices. Ami had become a vegetarian, identifying with her Jain ancestry, and I had moved away from Hindu rituals, and increasingly interested in Hindu philosophy (e.g., Vedanta, Bhagavad Gita).

The exploration of these issues was especially important as they were largely unspoken within our families. We were socialized to not speak about personal conflicts with those outside of our immediate families. However, the ability to talk about such conflicts with a friend with similar experiences was critical in developing a positive bicultural identity. Sometimes, it felt difficult to disclose to each other the negative feelings we had about our cultural background, such as social inequities that exist between men and women. Nonetheless, our friendship allowed for these negative, conflicted feelings to co-exist with what we loved most about our Indian culture, such as the warmth and informality of our community gatherings that was so consistently fostered by the aunties and uncles. We felt even more conflicted about sharing our experiences with family members, especially since we are both very close to our parents. We became accustomed to our parents telling us not disclose our family conflicts with our friends, and then choosing to tell each other anyway. In this way, our friendship became an act of resistance, as everything was open for discussion.

There have been contradictory perspectives on the role of cultural orientation on intimacy and self-disclosure. Some theorists (Castaneda & Burns-Glover, 2008) have suggested that intimacy and self-disclosure in friendship are more likely to occur in individualistic cultures when compared with interdependent cultures, whereas others (Alperin, 2001; Roland, 2006) view an individualistic orientation as posing challenges to intimacy due to its emphasis on competition, separation-individuation, and privacy. These perspectives can be expanded by attending to differences in immigrant generation. For second generation Asian Indians, a central conflict is negotiating across these individualistic and interdependent cultural frameworks as they develop friendships with similar and different ethnic backgrounds. The second generation struggles with a sense of belonging in multiple cultural contexts in a way that is distinct from the first generation. For first generation Asian Indians, similar ethnic social networks are critical sources of emotional and instrumental support in coping with acculturative stress (Mand, 2006). However, first generation and second generation Asian Indians typically vary with respect to disclosure of family conflicts and problems, particularly those related to mental health (Tummala-Narra, 2009). First generation Asian Indians tend to identify with the stigma against discussing psychological problems, while second generation Asian Indians tend to shift between disclosing these issues to their friends and maintaining privacy within the family. Both of these trajectories have implications for friendship formation, and for coping with psychological problems.

From the perspective of the second generation, friendships among the first generation may be perceived to be close and meaningful in some dimensions, but constricted in other ways. For the first generation, forming intimate relationships with friends in a way that involves self-disclosure about personal problems may be experienced as too risky, as they may fear that their children will not be accepted by the larger Indian community. The intergenerational conflicts between first and second generation is reflective of the demands of acculturation and transformation of cultural identifications. These conflicts raise questions of authenticity for each generation. For example, I struggled with how much of my emotional life to share with my parents and with my friends, sometimes feeling as though only pieces of my psyche were acceptable in each sphere. Winnicott (1986) noted the importance of being and feeling real as the basis for psychological health. The sense of realness for first and second generation can be compromised as the changes produced through immigration are denied or overlooked within and outside of the family, contributing to an "acculturation gap" (Prathikanti, 1997). Having a friendship at the hyphen (Indian-American) then becomes the holding environment (Winnicott, 1986) in which this denial can be confronted and new possibilities for identity emerge. This was the space in which my friendship with Ami unfolded.

WRITING OUR OWN SCRIPTS

Feminist scholars have emphasized how women's friendships provide a location for social change (Castaneda & Burns-Glover, 2008; Maroda, 2004). Emotional support from friends is empowering, and helps women cope with oppression such as sexism and racism. Experiences of discrimination contribute to emotional distress, and the internalization of negative self-images about the self and the physical body (e.g., skin color, hair texture, body shape) (Grabe & Hyde, 2006; Tummala-Narra, 2007; Takeuchi, Zane, Hong, Chae, Gong, Gee et al., 2007). For immigrant women, racism, sexism, homophobia, ableism, and classism contribute to acculturative stress. Experiences of discrimination within and outside of the ethnic community further complicate a sense of belonging in one's ethnic community and/or mainstream society (Comas-Diaz, 2008; Suarez-Orozco & Qin, 2006). The negative effects of immigration, such as social isolation, often go unnoticed as women function in stressful social conditions (e.g., balancing work family responsibilities, experiences of physical and sexual violence, lack of education and/or employment).

Women's access to friendships with other women is especially important in coping with and resisting oppression. Comas-Diaz (2008) eloquently described the importance of personal and social transformation among women of color as a way to critically address the psychological effects of colonization. Women's solidarity and prioritization of their friendships and connections with each other can actively challenge oppressive social expectations and internalized stereotypes of gender and race (Knickmeyer, Sexton, & Nishimura, 2002). In a sense, placing women's friendships at the center of social change is an act of resistance, and a validation of women's individual and collective power.

As many immigrants rely on similar ethnic social networks in coping with discrimination (Tummala-Narra, Inman, & Ettigi, 2011), Ami and I talked with each other and other Indian American friends in discussing and challenging stereotypes about Indians. In our early adulthood, we talked about how some people assumed that we were subservient to men in our families in part due to media images of Indian women. We continue to talk about the lack of representation and misrepresentation of Indian women and men in mainstream society, and what this can mean for our children. Throughout the years, I've come to rely on Ami as someone who can challenge these stereotypes, sometimes by speaking out against these stereotypes directly with those who offend us, and sometimes in private conversations where we express our sadness and anger. It is also worth noting that we have chosen professions in which we hope to foster change and heal others. Interestingly, neither one of us chose to become the stereotyped Indian doctor or engineer. I believe that we were drawn to our professions as a function of our role as healers in our families who worked to integrate broken and disavowed aspects of the immigrant experience. Working through these conflicts has been challenging and empowering.

Ami and I recently acknowledged that we are consciously working to help our children cope with stereotypes of Indians in ways that were not available to us as children. Hall and Fine (2005) have written about the positive side of marginality in which living on the outside and the inside creates strength and resistance to dominant distortions of women's subjective realities. Positive marginality entails writing and re-writing one's own scripts, independent of dominant messages. Ami and I have embraced our marginality and hyphenated identities, and encourage our children to do the same. In doing so, we have unknowingly discovered new possibilities for identity.

FRIENDSHIP IN THE CONTEXT OF CHANGE AND LOSS

While my relationships with friends have changed with time and circumstances, my friendship with Ami has matured over the years despite living in separate parts of the country. Throughout the years, we have called each other every week, eager to share our experiences. Ami and I continue to question, revisit, and reshape our identities as Indian American women. We talk about the challenges and joys of marriage, motherhood, and professional life. We talk about our relationships with our parents and siblings, and the fears of someday losing our parents, and perhaps our strongest connection with our Indian identity. We now identify with our parents' concerns about transmitting Indian cultural values and helping our children develop positive identifications with their Indian and American heritage. We have supported each other through the loss of loved ones in our families, and challenges to our children's physical health and that of our own. Our friendship is one that has offered a sense of continuity essential to coping with life transitions in a way that respects our multiple identities as Indian-American women.

Further, this friendship has been the space in which we have negotiated our separation from our mothers with whom we both have deeply identified. As in the case of many mother-daughter relationships (Maroda, 2004), our mothers encouraged us to be independent in our professional lives in the hope that we would achieve a sense of self-reliance that was not accessible to them. At the same time, they taught us to be devoted to our families. Ami and I consult each other regularly about how best to manage the demands of work and family, and how to enjoy experiences in both realms. We have encouraged each other to develop positive friendships with other women to create more "real" spaces where we can grow and reach out to others. When I moved away from Michigan, Ami encouraged me to find a meaningful life for myself and for my family. She understood that separation did not mean an ending or weakening of our friendship, but rather a necessary step for my growth. Perhaps, it is our familiarity with and personal work on the hyphen that has helped us to bear and negotiate separation and growth. From an intrapsychic perspective, she and I have known that our friendship would continue to thrive despite our separations (Harris, 2002).

THE HYPHEN, INTIMACY, AND PSYCHOTHERAPY

Western psychotherapy is an unfamiliar path of healing for many immigrants. I had decided to become a clinical psychologist during a time that it was considered both an unusual and undesirable occupation within the Asian Indian community, even though I felt supported by my parents. The fact that I am a woman made it somewhat more acceptable, however, as I was expected to eventually place more emphasis on my family life than my career. The ambivalent reception of my career choice was complicated by my experiences in graduate training, where there was little mention of the role of cultural differences in psychopathology and psychotherapy. Although I had developed a good foundation in cognitive-behavioral and psychoanalytic models, I left graduate school not knowing how to integrate my cultural identity and life experiences in my professional life. Throughout this time, I often felt isolated, and reached out to family and friends as a way to refuel myself. Again, I was on the margins, negotiating my hyphenated identity.

Over the years, my immersion into feminist, multicultural, and relational psychoanalytic frameworks helped me to bridge these gaps in psychological theory and practice. Feminist and multicultural perspectives (Brown, 2005; Comas-Diaz, 2008; Greene, 2008) challenged traditional conceptualizations of the therapeutic relationship. Together, these perspectives focus on dynamics of power, social hierarchies and inequities, and cultural dynamics that shape the therapeutic relationship. The therapist takes an egalitarian, empowering, and culturally sensitive approach that respects the client's own sensibility about his/her treatment. Psychoanalytic developments in the past two decades have centered on the relational context of psychotherapy. Feminist psychoanalytic theorists (Chodorow, 1999; Kristeva, 1982) have questioned traditional concepts of gender and cultural experience, highlighting the influence of patriarchal beliefs in the therapeutic process. Drawing on the relational and intersubjective psychoanalytic models (Mitchell, 1993; Stolorow, 2002), some psychoanalytic scholars (Altman, 2010; Tummala-Narra, 2009; Yi, 1998) have raised attention to the role of subjectivity of sociocultural location in the therapeutic relationship. Transference, in this framework, is thought to be co-constructed by therapist and client, and mirrors dynamics rooted in social hierarchies outside of the psychotherapy context. Overlapping with feminist and multicultural paradigms (Barrett, Chin, Comas-Diaz, Espin, Greene, & McGoldrick, 2005), this perspective argues for a close examination of cultural norms in the formulation of pathology and health (Yi, 1998; Roland, 2006). In my own clinical practice, an integration of these perspectives has helped me to attend to my clients' social and cultural realities, and to the conscious and unconscious meanings of these realities (Tummala-Narra, 2009). This integration has also contributed to an understanding of intimacy in the therapeutic relationship that considers the ways that social context shapes wishes and fears of closeness and belonging. The following case vignette illustrates how feminist, multicultural, and psychodynamic concepts inform a conceptualization of intimacy within a three-year-long psychotherapy with a second generation Iraqi American client.

CASE ILLUSTRATION

Catherine is a 55-year-old married, heterosexual woman of a Chaldean Christian, Iraqi background. Her parents were born and raised in Iraq, and they immigrated to the U.S. four years prior to Catherine's birth. She has one younger sister. She and her husband are both employed. When she initially contacted me, she expressed that she was experiencing marital conflict, and that she was worried about her 25-year-old daughter who was coping with depression. She described her marriage as unhappy and difficult, as she had frequent verbal arguments with her husband, usually centered on financial strain and conflicts related to how best to help their daughter. Catherine hoped to get help in addressing her family conflicts.

Catherine's upbringing involved a close connection with her Chaldean community. As a young girl, she identified strongly with Chaldean Christian cultural and religious values. Chaldeans are Catholic Christians with roots in Iraq, with a collectivistic orientation that values connection with immediate and extended family and larger ethnic and religious community. Men are typically experienced as the head of households, and the notion of discussing emotional problems outside of the family is often stigmatized (Hakim-Larson, Kamoo, Nassar-McMillan, & Porcerelli, 2007). As in the case of many immigrant communities (e.g., Asian and Latino/a), Chaldean Americans cope with acculturative stress and intergenerational conflicts among family members.

Catherine described her parents' adjustment to living in the United States as stressful, and that while women in the Chaldean community tended not have as much power relative to men, she felt that these roles were actually reversed in the case of her parents. She stated that her mother was "demanding and overpowering" in comparison with her father. Catherine described her relationship with her mother as distant. She stated that her mother was overly concerned with her own physical appearance and social status within the Chaldean community, and that she behaved more as a peer than her mother. On the other hand, she felt close to her father who apparently was more attentive to her and her sister. Sadly, her father died suddenly due to illness when she was an adolescent. Catherine recalled being grief-stricken, and that she coped with her loss by emotionally moving away from her family and her community. Her distance from her mother grew, particularly after her mother remarried. Although Catherine came to care about her stepfather, whom she describes as loving and kind, she continued to experience her mother as self-focused. During her mid-adolescence, Catherine worked to fit in socially at school and at times felt different because of her Chaldean background and because she had suffered the loss of her father, which few people outside of her home had noticed. She soon began dating a boy whom she describes as her "first love," and when this relationship ended two years later, she felt devastated. Soon after this break-up, she met and married her husband. Her description of her husband as a "good man" seemed to lack a feeling of romantic connection.

The psychotherapeutic work initially focused on Catherine's concerns about her daughter who eventually was able to seek help for her depression. While she was able to talk about her concerns for her daughter, she had difficulty speaking about her own emotional experiences in relating with important people in her life, such as her daughter, husband, and mother. She would state, "Well, that is just how it is, and I just have to accept it." Her devotion to her marriage was reinforced by her religious beliefs about marital commitment. As the treatment progressed, Catherine reluctantly talked about her relationship with her husband. She had never felt a strong emotional connection with him, such as the one she experienced with her first boyfriend in adolescence. She expressed feeling guilty and responsible for her marital conflicts, and made great efforts to "make the relationship work" by initiating interactions with her husband. Yet, she felt a deep sense of loneliness.

Catherine's connection with her sister played a critical role in her ability to cope with her emotional stress. Since her early adulthood, her sister had been her best friend, and a confidante with whom she could discuss joy, disappointment and loss. They shared a mutual experience of their mother as difficult and emotionally inaccessible. Her sister who was married and had no children of her own adopted a maternal role with Catherine's daughter. She was especially helpful during times when Catherine was unable to bear her daughter's distress. Although Catherine felt a strong bond with her sister, she worried that her sister would disapprove of her if she talked more openly about her marital conflicts. Toward the end of the first year of psychotherapy, Catherine took the risk of talking with her sister, after feeling increasingly unhappy in her marriage. To her relief, her sister was supportive to her and asked her to consider couples psychotherapy. Catherine had also begun to take risks in the therapeutic relationship. For the first time in our work together, she asked if we could meet more frequently, perhaps twice a week. She qualified her request by letting me know that she would understand if I did not have time in my schedule. I responded by thanking her for asking for what she wanted and needed. For the next year, we worked in twice-weekly psychotherapy.

Catherine gradually began to express her feelings of anger toward the people she loved. Prior to this, she treaded carefully in her intimate relationships. She consciously tried to "keep the conversations light" in her interactions with friends, daughter, husband, and parents. She worried about burdening others with her stress. This cautious approach was also evident in our relationship when she conveyed her concern for me as a working mother. She stated in one session, "I don't know how you can work evening hours. You must be tired. It's hard to be away from your kids." In these moments, I wondered whether Catherine was defensively focused on my life as a mother as a way to avoid talking about her own distress. At the same time, I recognized that Catherine may have been trying to engage in a reciprocal process in which she could experience herself in the familiar position of caretaking. I understood these interactions as her attempts to know me better and to feel closer to me. When I raised this as a possibility, Catherine stated that her wish to care for others was related to both her role in her family and to her personal religious and cultural values. She imagined that I would understand this perspective since I am from an immigrant background. I told her that I can relate to being of immigrant origin, and that I had hoped to learn more about what her immigrant background meant for her. Catherine then talked about the challenges of the hyphen experience, especially of shifting across different cultural context, and of not feeling fully like herself in any one context.

I wondered about other possibilities with respect to Catherine's transference. On one hand, her transference seemed to reflect her wish to connect with me as a sister, or perhaps a nurturing maternal figure for whom she longed. On the other hand, I experienced her transference as involving disappointment toward me for not being with my children in the evening, the inaccessible mother with whom she was familiar. I asked her to tell me more about her wish to connect with me. She responded by saying that it felt difficult to talk about herself, and she was unsure of what she wanted in her relationships. She worried about depending on her sister too much, even though she enjoyed and thrived in their friendship. Later in our work, she was able to talk about how she worried about depending on me.

Catherine's dilemmas of intimacy were rooted in layers of emotional experiences that had not been accessible to her since childhood. She adapted to her losses by creating emotional distance to avoid consciously experiencing empathic failures by her caregivers. While this approach helped her cope with her grief, it restricted her from experiencing emotional intimacy with others, and from knowing herself more fully. Psychoanalytic scholars (Luepnitz, 2002) have noted that while definitions of love, intimacy, aggression, and privacy vary across social location (e.g. social class, culture), the experience of ambivalence in balancing the concern for the self and that for others is one that is shared across context. Catherine's approach to intimacy was shaped by early experiences with her mother connected with her Chaldean Christian background. She viewed her mother as non-traditional and as someone who didn't conform to their cultural norms and traditions. For Catherine, this non-conformity was closely aligned with her mother's self-focused position. She stated that she sometimes felt embarrassed that her mother stood out in community gatherings, and paid more attention to her own dress and appearance than that of her children. As a mother, Catherine had been more successful in attending to her daughter's needs, and in psychotherapy, came to recognize that her daughter had been able to reveal her struggles to her in ways that Catherine could not have imagined doing with her own mother. Catherine also worked hard to retain her cultural and religious beliefs, in part to write her own script. She wanted to be the woman and mother that her mother was not. While she valued the collectivistic nature of her cultural background, at times, she recognized that her wish to be a "good, Chaldean mom" came at a cost to her own voice. She tended to suppress painful feelings about her marriage, and the growing distance from her husband.

Catherine's struggles with intimacy gradually led to her taking the risk to explore and explicitly express her thoughts, feelings, and wishes. She talked about the difficulty of bearing ambivalence and contradictory feelings (e.g., love, anger, disappointment) about her family and friends. In psychoanalytic theory (Alperin, 2001; Winnicott, 1986), the recognition of negative and positive feelings about the self and others is thought to be essential for intimacy and authenticity. Intimacy in the psychotherapeutic relationship develops through the subjectivity of the therapist and the client, and as such, Catherine's "knowing" herself was a function of our independent and collective understanding of her experiences. Dimen (2010) described the interplay of subjectivity and the fluid nature of insight in psychotherapy: "It is less the analyst's certain knowledge than the analyst's ongoing effort to understand that makes the difference" (p. 255). In this view, insight emerges from the intersubjective space between the therapist and the client, and therapeutic change occurs in the relational context.

In our last year of working together, Catherine had confirmed her fear that her husband had been involved with someone else. As she increasingly talked with her sister about her marital stress, her sister supported her and encouraged her to confront him. Catherine was both deeply saddened and relieved when she asked her husband about the affair. She decided to separate from her husband, and later filed for divorce. She stayed with her sister for a period of time as she felt that she could now be completely at home with her. Her sister was instrumental in helping her to cope with this loss, and the accompanying anxiety related to her identity as a Chaldean woman who had decided to end her marriage. In describing her sister's support through the divorce, Catherine stated, "I feel like I have a witness." Although the ending of her marriage was deeply painful, Catherine would tell me that she felt more like who she really is. She said, "I always knew this (marriage) wasn't going to work, and now I can finally say it." Catherine had begun to find her voice, and to experience ambivalence in her relationships, without only fearing loss and abandonment. Further, being and feeling real with her sister and with me allowed her to feel more authentic in her relationship with her daughter. The process of writing her own script felt powerful to her. In our work, we shifted across multiple identities (e.g., cultural, religious, immigrant, mother), some which were Catherine's and some which were mine, eventually creating a space in which she came to hear herself and take the risk to be heard.

LESSONS LEARNED

I have attempted in this article to illustrate the healing power of women's friendships and relationships with each other. I believe that my friendship with Ami has helped me to learn more about intimacy and authenticity, which are essential aspects of the psychotherapeutic relationship. Immigrant women's negotiation of the hyphen takes place in a relational context that can bear ambivalence, loss, similarity and difference. I shared Catherine's dilemmas concerning cultural identity and relationships with family members. At the same time, I recognize the unique meaning of these dilemmas, and life circumstances that shape each of our experiences. Friendship and intimacy, while universal needs, are constructed through social context and the meanings attached to this context. As I reflect on my friendships with female friends, I have noted the following lessons that are relevant for effective psychotherapy practice.

1. The therapist's approach to intimacy in her personal life must be well understood. As relationships with family and friends provide a template for intimacy in adulthood, it is especially important the therapist is aware of how her own conflicts with intimacy may influence the therapeutic process. An effective therapeutic relationship is one in which positive and negative experiences of the self and other are explored, making space for greater authenticity (Dimen, 2010).
2. Friendship can provide a safe space for exploring complex, contradictory feelings about the self and others. As such, the therapist should explore the client's friendships, how they have changed over time, and how they have influenced identity. The therapist should consider that clients of immigrant origin often rely on similar ethnic friendships as they form a bicultural identity. Friendships can be a source of women's resilience in meeting the demands of multiple identifications with family, community, and cultural context (Greene, 2008). Additionally, it is important to note the fluid nature of the hyphen and the ways in which friendship transforms identity over time and circumstance.
3. It is important that the therapist explore her social location (e.g., age, race, gender, culture, social class, sexual orientation, religion/spirituality, dis/ability) and its relevance to friendship and intimacy in order to understand the influence of social context on the client's relational life. The therapist can then recognize power dynamics that are based in social differences within the therapeutic relationship (Altman, 2010; Tummala-Narra, 2007). The acknowledgement of racism, sexism, and other forms of oppression can be a critical source of validation for women's experiences.

The therapeutic relationship, much like a friendship, involves bearing witness and sharing voice. Psychoanalytic theorists have described the importance of the therapist's respect and love for the client as essential to meaningful change (Glucksman, 2010; Novick and Novick, 2000). While traditional psychological theories of intervention have focused on the therapist's objectivity and neutrality, women's experiences speak to the importance of the relational context in therapeutic change and to the unique set of social realities that shape relational life.

REFERENCES

Akhtar, S. (2011). *Immigration and acculturation: Mourning, adaptation, and the next generation.* New York: Jason Aronson.

Alperin, R. M. (2001). Barriers to intimacy: An object relations perspective. *Psychoanalytic Psychology, 18*(1), 137–156.

Barrett, S. E., Chin, J. L., Comas-Diaz, L., Espin, O., Greene, B., & McGoldrick, M. (2005). Multicultural feminist therapy: Theory in context. *Women & Therapy, 28*(3/4), 27–61.

Brown, L. S. (2010). *Feminist therapy.* Washington, D.C.: American Psychological Association.

Castaneda, D., & Burns-Glover, A. L. (2008). Women's friendships and romantic relationships. In F.L. Denmark & M.A. Paludi (Eds.), *Psychology of women: A handbook of issues and theories (2nd ed.)* (pp. 332–350). Westport, CT: Praeger Publishers/Greenwood Publishing Group.

Chodorow, N. J. (1999). *The power of feelings: Personal meaning in psychoanalysis, gender, and culture.* New Haven, CT: Yale University Press.

Comas-Diaz, L. (2008). 2007 Carolyn Wood Sherif Award Address: Spirita: Reclaiming womanist sacredness into feminism. *Psychology of Women Quarterly, 32*, 13–21.

Dimen, M. (2010). Reflections on cure, or "I/Thou/It." *Psychoanalytic Dialogues, 20*, 254–268.

Glucksman, M. L. (2010). Is love curative? *Journal of the American Academy of Psychoanalysis and Dynamic Psychiatry, 38*(1), 159–179.

Grabe, S., & Hyde, J. S. (2006). Ethnicity and body dissatisfaction among women in the United States: A meta-analysis. *Psychological Bulletin, 132*(4), 622–640.

Greene, B. (2008). African American women, religion, and oppression: The use and abuse of spiritual beliefs. In C. A. Rayburn & L. Comas-Diaz (Eds.), *Womansoul: The inner life of women's spirituality* (pp. 153–166). Westport, CT: Praeger.

Hakim-Larson, J., Kamoo, R., Nassar-McMillan, S. C., & Porcerelli, J. H. (2007). Counseling Arab and Chaldean American families. *Journal of Mental Health Counseling, 29*(4), 301–321.

Hall, R. L., & Fine, M. (2005). The stories we tell: The lives and friendship of two older Black lesbians. *Psychology of Women Quarterly, 29*, 177–187.

Harris, A. (2002). Mothers, monsters, mentors. *Studies in gender and sexuality, 3*(3), 281–295.

Knickmeyer, N., Sexton, K., & Nishimura, N. (2002). The impact of same-sex friendships on the well-being of women: A review of the literature. *Women & Therapy, 25*(1), 37–59.

Kristeva, J. (1982). *Powers of horror: An essay on abjection.* New York, NY: Columbia University.

Little, G. (1989). Freud, friendship, and politics. In R. Porter & S. Tomaselli (eds.), *The dialectics of friendship* (pp. 143–158). London: Routledge.

Luepnitz, D. A. (2002). *Schopenhauer's porcupines: Intimacy and its dilemmas.* New York: Basic Books.

Mand, K. (2006). Social relations beyond the family? Exploring elderly South Asian women's friendships in London. *Community, Work, and Family, 9*(3), 309–323.

Maroda, K. J. (2004). A relational perspective on women and power. *Psychoanalytic Psychology, 21*(3), 428–435.

Miller, J. B., & Stiver, I. P. (1997). *The healing connection: How women form relationships in therapy and in life.* Boston, MA: Beacon Press.

Mitchell, S. A. (1993). *Hope and dread in psychoanalysis.* New York: Basic Books.

O'Connor, P. (1992). *Friendships between women.* New York: Guilford Press.

Prathi Kanti, S. (1997). East Indian American families. In E. Lee (Ed.), *Working with Asian Americans: A guide for Clinicians* (pp. 79–100). New York, NY: Guilford.

Roland, A. (2006). Across civilizations: Psychoanalytic therapy with Asians and Asian Americans. *Psychotherapy: Theory, Research, Practice, Training, 43*(4), 454–463.

Sirin, S. R., & Fine, M. (2007). Hyphenated selves: Muslim American youth negotiating on the fault lines of global conflict. *Applied Developmental Science, 11*(3), 151–163.

Stolorow, R. D. (2002). From drive to affectivity: Contextualizing psychological life. *Psychoanalytic Inquiry, 22,* 678–685.

Suarez-Orozco, C., & Qin, B. (2006). Gendered perspectives in psychology: Immigrant origin youth. *IMR, 40*(1), 165–198.

Takeuchi, D. T., Zane, N., Hong, S., Chae, D. H., Gong, F., Gee, G. C., Walton, E., Sue, S., & Alegria, M. (2007). Immigration-related factors and mental disorders among Asian Americans. *American Journal of Public Health, 97*(1), 84–90.

Tummala-Narra, P. (2007). Skin color and the therapeutic relationship. *Psychoanalytic Psychology, 24*(2), 255–270.

Tummala-Narra, P. (2009). The immigrant's real and imagined return home. Psychoanalysis, *Culture & Society,14,* 237–252.

Tummala-Narra, P., Inman, A. G., & Ettigi, S. (2011). Asian Indians' Responses to Discrimination: A mixed-method examination of identity, coping, and self-esteem. *Asian American Journal of Psychology, 2*(3), 205–218.

Winnicott, D. W. (1986). *Home is where we start from: Essays by a psychoanalyst.* New York: W.W. Norton.

Yi, K. Y. (1998). Transference and race: An intersubjective conceptualization. *Psychoanalytic Psychology, 15*(2), 245–261.

Hermanas de Corazón y Alma

CARRIE L. CASTAÑEDA-SOUND
Pepperdine University, Encino, California

Friendship is a relationship that can traverse generations or be located within a specific era of a person's life. In this article, the author examines the role that her childhood friendship played in shaping her understanding of gender, ethnicity, poverty, immigration, spirituality and family processes. This friendship was during emerging adolescence and helped the author navigate and develop mestiza consciousness. These lessons were reinforced during her graduate training and have influenced her identity as a Chicana feminist therapist and the manner in which she connects with clients in psychotherapy. After presenting the story of her friendship, the author incorporates the theoretical perspectives of Chicana Feminism and Spirita to demonstrate how this friendship has influenced her clinical work with women. Specific themes discussed are language, invisibility, and cultural formulations of gender and spirituality.

INTRODUCTION

> *"A bosom friend—an intimate friend, you know—a really kindred spirit to whom I can confide my inmost soul. I've dreamed of meeting her all my life."*

The bosom friend described by the orphaned Anne in the children's book *Anne of Green Gables* (Montgomery, 1908, p. 64) resonated with my dream to have a confidant to share my deepest secrets. Carmen Lopez was just that for me—the kindred spirit I am so grateful I met at the age of 12. Our friendship has waxed and waned since our adolescence in the early 1980s until now, but a common thread throughout it all is the love and soulful bond described so eloquently by Anne. Through this complex relationship, I have learned first-hand about authenticity, spirituality, and the many roads to ethnic and gender identity within the context of poverty and family processes. Not only have these lessons influenced my growth as a woman and friend, but also my clinical work as a Chicana feminist therapist. I will present our friendship story and application to my clinical work within the theoretical lenses of *Spirita,* "... a womanist and *mujerista* spirituality" (Comas-Diaz, 2008, p. 13), and Chicana feminism, which "... is a move away from silence, giving voice to our experience" (Córdova, 1998, p. 38).

NUESTRO ENCUENTRO

At the age of 12, my parents decided to transfer me from a religious private school to a public school in the suburbs of Los Angeles, California. Unfortunately the day of this transfer was in the middle of the school year, and the first day at my new public school was on Valentine's Day. I dreaded that first day, and my fears were realized when I observed the students exchanging gifts and cards. During my last class of the day, Carmen Lopez introduced herself and shared one of her Valentine lollipops with me. She had long black hair, a soft voice not unlike my own, and a sweet smile. I later learned that this smile was reserved only for the most deserving, for she was skilled at reading her surroundings and determining the authenticity of people she met. This sense of intuition was a survival skill that was refined throughout her life, and was necessary in our small town that had few Latino families.

Carmen was my first "best friend." I was extremely shy as a pre-teen; consequently making new friends was not easy for me. I preferred to read my books and play sports, but the thought of initiating friendships was terrifying. We both enjoyed reading, listening to typical teen music, and excelling in our classes. We even created a secret diary that contained our favorite poems, lyrics from songs we loved, and dreams for our future. We could be real with each other, and within the space of unconditional love, we were able to share our deepest fears, pain, and joy.

FAMILIA (FAMILY)

Although we were kindred spirits, our families were profoundly different and this friendship offered me my first glimpse into the powerful role family processes play in individuals' lives. To teachers and friends unfamiliar with

Latino culture, we seemed to come from similar backgrounds as Mexican Americans. On the contrary, we came from very different worlds. We experienced *mestiza consciousness* (Anzaldúa, 1987) in different ways. Anzaldúa (1987) describes this consciousness as living in the Borderlands of multiple cultures, with the ability of the *mestiza* to "... sustain contradictions, she turns the ambivalence into something else" (p. 101).

Carmen's parents were born in Mexico and immigrated to the United States to work and raise their family, whereas I came from a bi-ethnic and bi-cultural family with a long history in California and Arizona. While I had numerous relatives in the surrounding area, Carmen's extended family remained in Mexico. She spoke Spanish daily with her parents, whereas my exposure to Spanish was reserved for visits with my grandparents and relatives. Even within these differences we found connections. We both shared a love of *familia*, but the expression of our dedication looked very different. Her dedication was expressed daily in very culturally defined gender roles. Not only was she expected to help her mother with household work, but she also was expected to act as her mother's culture and language broker (see Morales & Hanson, 2005; Orellana, Dorner, & Pulido, 2003) when her father was at work. The role of language broker was very time consuming and began the moment she returned from school. I often accompanied Carmen and Mrs. Lopez on less-intrusive excursions to the supermarket and post office; but I was not invited when Carmen assisted her mother at doctor appointments or visits to the welfare or immigration office. Privacy was superseded by the needs of the family within the Lopez household. As language broker, Carmen was present when her mother learned of very personal information, such as a tumor that was feared to be cancerous. Carmen was not permitted the luxury of her emotional reaction, for she had to focus on the task at hand. She had to access the correct vocabulary to interpret the information from English to Spanish, and she had to be sure to ask her mother's questions as well as her own. Because she felt like she had to be strong for her parents, the fear and sadness were only expressed in our diary.

Carmen asked me to keep our secret diary at my house because she was afraid to take it home. She feared her parents would take it away and not allow her to have these secrets. I quickly learned that Carmen's parents were stricter than my own, and she did not enjoy the freedoms that I enjoyed. She often complained that her parents would not allow her to participate in extracurricular activities. She explained to me that her parents had the dream that she would get a scholarship to college and become a doctor. Our parents were not dissimilar in this respect, but my parents also valued the social experiences of high school.

The Lopez' style of parenting can be understood within more recent advances in the psychological literature about parenting. The parenting literature is shaped by the influential works of Baumrind (1966) and Maccoby and Martin (1983) and their development of the authoritarian, authoritative, neglectful, and permissive parenting styles. Empirical research generally supports these labels, yet few studies examined their applicability in Latino families. In a critical study with 50 first-generation Latino parents and their children, Domenech Rodríguez, Donovick, and Crowley (2009) included observational methods to understand parenting styles. These researchers included Baumrind's (1966) dimension of autonomy granting, which was typically not included parenting research. Results indicated that 61% of Latino parents could be categorized as "Protective." Specifically, they were characterized as high on warmth and demandingness, but low on autonomy granting. In addition, parents were lower on autonomy granting with their daughters compared with their sons. These data are descriptive of Carmen's parents and their style of parenting. They were very warm and loving, yet they were very strict about monitoring her activities outside of school. Clearly they held traditional values of *marianismo*, emulating the Virgin Mary and sacrificing for the family (Niemann, 2004). Brenda often complained about the inequities between her and her younger brothers. Her brothers were allowed much more latitude in both their physical movement between their home and the outside world, and the same freedom was applied to their emotional expression. Whereas Carmen was expected to be even-tempered, her brothers were permitted to be loud in laughter and in anger.

Interpreting the parental protection of Carmen only using a gendered lens would miss a very important dimension of their experience as undocumented immigrants. They trusted Carmen and believed she would make good choices, but that was irrelevant because they did not trust the world they lived in. After high school, Carmen shared with me that she was taught to disclose little about their family to "outsiders," or it might put the family in jeopardy of being deported. Another concern was that outside the boundaries of their family, the fear of attracting violence was a daily reality. They lived in a one-bedroom apartment in a neighborhood that was known for gang activity. Because of this, my parents forbade me to spend time with Carmen outside of school unless it was at my house in a "safe" neighborhood.

Ironically, when we were 13, we learned that a young woman was raped at a house two blocks from my home. My parents would not disclose the details, but I had to walk past this house daily on my way to and from school. Until this point in my life, my awareness of sexual assault and rape was nonexistent. In fact, my knowledge of sex was limited to pieces of information from television, music, and conversations with friends that were accompanied by embarrassed giggles. Both Carmen and I felt the impact of this assault on a visceral level. When we approached the house, we crossed the street, and our conversation ceased. In unison, we broke into a run until we reached the end of the block. Unconsciously we realized that just the fact that we were young girls put us at risk for harm, and we hadn't developed the tools (i.e., language) to make sense of this. No words were spoken, but the run empowered us.

POVERTY AND TRADITION

My parents worked outside the home, and my dad often worked two jobs at one time; we were considered a "working class" family. Carmen's family, however, was barely making it day to day. Mr. Lopez worked in the field of building construction, but he always was the first employee let go when business slowed down. Consequently, he worked any job he could find and often earned minimum wage or less. Mrs. Lopez stayed home and cared for Carmen and her younger brothers, and it wasn't until after high school that I learned that Mr. and Mrs. Lopez had a fifth grade reading level in Spanish, and struggled with learning to speak and write English. Their sense of connection with the community was through attendance at church functions through the Hispanic ministry. I went with their family to Sunday mass and always was in awe of the pride they had in their religious traditions. This was their connection to their culture and family in Mexico. Before every service, Carmen's mother prayed at the large painting of *La Virgin de Guadalupe.* I watched her bend on her knees and fervently pray. My adolescent mind could not grasp her dedication, but I knew and felt that I was in the presence of something very powerful. Even on her knees, I knew her strength and I saw the powerful calm that enveloped her during and after that prayer. Everyone knew that was her time, her time with the *Virgin*, but most importantly her time to be herself in connection with the divine. No one dared interrupt her.

The Lopez family always contributed to the weekly collection, and made this a priority. I was ashamed the first time I forgot my wallet at home and had no money to contribute. Even at the tender age of 13, I understood that I had privileges. At school, I knew Carmen was embarrassed that she received a free hot lunch. Even though I brought my lunch from home, I walked with her through the lunch line and chatted with her to distract her and anyone else nearby. I knew the look in Carmen's eyes when issues of money arose. She lost the twinkle in her eye, and she acted like she didn't care about whatever would cost her parents extra money. She was a great actress, but I knew my friend, and through her I learned about the shame of poverty.

IMPACT OF FRIENDSHIP ON PSYCHOTHERAPY WITH WOMEN

As an early-career professional, I look forward to my continued growth as a clinician. I have always been drawn to the inclusiveness and flexibility encouraged in feminist therapy. Brown (2010) explains,

> Today, feminist therapy continues to be founded theoretically in a close and careful analysis of the meanings and contributions of gender and

> other social locations such as culture, phenotype, social class, sexual orientation, and age, both to normative identity development and life trajectories as well as to the etiologies of distress and dysfunction. (p. 3)

Feminist therapy is congruent with the way I understand the world and the problems in it, and I use it as a framework for the integration of theories from critical psychology (Brown, 2010). Living in California, and previously in South Texas, the majority of my clients immigrated from Mexico or Central America, and received therapy in community mental health settings that offered a sliding-fee schedule. Their presenting problems often were depression or anxiety, and these concerns were exacerbated by struggles to find a Spanish-speaking therapist. An example of this systemic barrier to treatment includes agencies that have bilingual therapists but have no Spanish-speaking staff to answer phones. As a result, when clients need to contact their therapist, they must follow special rules such as only calling on a specific day, or calling after hours to leave a message in Spanish. Upon our first meeting, my clients are often very relieved to learn that not only am I Latina, but I understand Spanish.

Although the "presenting problems" tend to be intrapsychic/individual in nature, our work invariably turns to themes about language, voice, understanding, and invisibility. González (2001) shares her own awareness as a child that her grandmother did not speak English, "I could not fathom that *she did not speak English*. Even in my immature state, I could discern that a person who did not speak English was invisible. He or she did not exist. English was the currency of exchange for securing personhood" (p. 50).

Based on my experiences with Carmen and her mother, I have learned that this invisibility takes a toll on an individual. Speaking in my client's first language, coupled with an authentic and respectful acceptance sets a powerful context for a woman who feels marginalized linguistically, ethnically, and sexually. For example, the simple comment "*No entiendo inglés* (I don't understand English)," can easily be transformed to "*No entienden español* (They don't understand Spanish)." This small transformation shifts agency for problems in communication and the identified source of deficiency in a way that gives clients a new perspective of their problem as external from themselves.

Much of the research about bilingual therapy and the shift to the dominant language to access deep emotions discuss the problems that may be encountered if the client "resists" by switching back to English (Aguirre, Bermúdez, Cardona, Zamora, & Reyes, 2005; Altarriba & Santiago-Rivera, 1994; Bond & Lai, 1986; Clauss, 1998). Rather than view this as "resistance," I experience this as a method of coping and a sense of reclaiming their experience. As a clinician, this is a sign that we have moved too quickly. While it would seem that this would be empowering for the client, some bilingual clients avoid speaking in Spanish, because it is associated with feelings of vulnerability. Language then becomes a variable in the therapeutic process of healing, and with a feminist perspective is modulated by the client.

For example, Isabel was a 40-year-old Mexican American woman who I worked with in individual counseling regarding a traumatic event in which she thought her 17-year-old son had died. She recalled that her son was changing the oil in his car in front of their house, while she was in the kitchen preparing dinner. She said she heard a loud crash from the front yard, and immediately knew something was wrong. She said she rushed to the front yard to see that a large truck had smashed into her son's car and it was demolished. All she could imagine was her son's body hidden within the folds of the crushed metal. She said she screamed and ran to the car looking for her son. She said she felt like she was outside herself and wondered who was screaming so loud. Later she realized it was her. She recounted that her husband ran out and grabbed her, but she was trying to pull away and look for her son. She recalled feeling so angry that her husband was not helping her but was instead fighting her. What seemed like hours were only minutes until she could hear her husband's voice. He was telling her that their son was not in the accident. He was explaining that their son used the family car to go to the store to buy materials for the oil change, and that he was safe. Isabel shared that even though her son was safe, she could not move on. She said she could barely get out of bed every day and that she felt "depressed." She also felt guilty because she had two younger children that still needed her, but she was struggling with day-to-day life. She added that her husband was concerned about her and urged her to seek therapy.

The first month of our work together was in English. We discussed language in the first session when I overheard her talk to her young child in Spanish. I offered that she could speak in Spanish in our sessions, but she quickly denied that as an option. As I got to know her better, I noticed an emotional shift when she spoke about the event. She seemed very detached and somewhat robotic. When we explored her network of support, she explained that she no longer felt safe driving, so her *Tía* (aunt) drives her everywhere. She added that they take daily walks together. When I asked about these walks, she shyly shared that they walk to the Catholic Church together to pray. She added that her *Tía* waits in the lobby while we are in session. I asked if she would like her *Tía* to a join a session, and Isabel happily agreed. She shared that she would like for us to meet. During our meeting with *Tía Elia*, I was surprised to learn that she preferred to speak in Spanish. She immediately began talking about her love for Isabel and with tears in her eyes, shared that she hopes Isabel will become whole again. I asked her to explain what she means by this, and she said she felt that Isabel had experienced *susto* (fright), and that her soul had left her body and was lost. She said she had encouraged Isabel to go to a *curandera* (traditional female healer) for a *limpia* (cleansing), but that Isabel no longer believes in the "old" ways of healing. When I turned to Isabel, I was surprised to see tears flowing down her face, and I asked her in Spanish what she was feeling. She replied in Spanish that she agreed that it felt like her soul was gone, but that she is not sure how to get it back. Much of our subsequent work was in Spanish and English and we used the metaphor of *llamando* (calling) her soul back and feeling whole. She shared that therapy, prayer, and the daily walks helped, and we often talked about the demnads of her role as *madre y esposa,* (mother and wife). We often discussed the elder women in her life as guides for how she could feel empowered. Often this involved re-defining *mujer (woman)* as powerful. For example, Isabel felt validated by the reconceptualization of her fright not as a deficit, or that it was due to her weakness; but as a reflection of her innermost power, and that her soul needed to be protected. Also, with the help of her *Tía Elia,* she found a reputable curandera to conduct a *limpia* and help her along in her process of re-connection with her soul.

The concept of *Spirita* is an appropriate application to Isabel's experience, in that it allows for multiple influences of healing and power, and the integration of traditional religion and indigenous approaches (Comas-Diaz, 2008). Isabel shared that she appreciated that during the *limpia,* her *curandera* used traditional prayers to God. The *curandera* compared Isabel's love of her son to the love the *Virgin de Guadalupe* felt for her son. *La Virgin de Guadalupe* is considered the patron saint of the Americas, and as described by Comas-Diaz (2008, p. 18) is a "... syncretism of the Aztec goddess Tonantzin with the Christian Virgin Mary, Guadalupe constitutes a spiritual paradox (Castillo, 1996). Even though Guadalupe is a small, dark, and poor *mestiza,* she is a most powerful freedom fighter (Teish, 1996)." The smooth transitions from weakness and fright to powerful fighter became the final themes of Isabel's healing narrative; but congruent with *Spirita,* they were not accomplished alone, but in solidarity with her community of *mujeres* (women).

SELF-REFLECTION

Working from the perspectives of Chicana feminism and *Spirita* allow me to access my clients' framework for understanding the world, and acknowledge their strengths as they navigate their healing paths. Just as my friend Carmen was imbued with the gift of intuition about people and her surroundings, I am not surprised when women of color share such talents. Like Carmen, I was raised in a family that valued and feared the supernatural. Dreams provided the opportunity to communicate with loved ones that transitioned to the afterlife, superstitions were carefully followed, but most importantly instinctual feelings and thoughts were honored. Comas-Diaz (2008) validates these *gifts of power,*

> Contrary to mainstream psychology, indigenous psychologies acknowledge spirituality as a form of knowledge, method, and development.

> Indeed, one of the ways that Eurocentric psychology attempts to colonize women of color is through the degradation of their spiritual experiences. Within this framework, gifts of power constitute a resistance against oppression, colonization, and cultural imperialism. (p. 17)

My friendship with Carmen Lopez enriched my life, but also made me aware of a profound loss. When I first met Carmen's family and saw how different they were from my own, I thought my Mexican heritage had been lost through the generations. The academic term is acculturation, yet this word does not come close to the felt grief of the gradual loss of language and cultural traditions. While Carmen wanted to be more American, I wanted to be more *Mexicana*. Our friendship took us to the midpoint where we learned about being bicultural and shifting identities.

Both Carmen and I continue to live in the Borderlands of ethnic and gender identity. With our higher education and interests in ethnic and gender studies, we both can deconstruct our experiences of socialization, yet we still struggle with the discomfort of these new lenses. As mothers, we are now in the role of teaching our children re-visioned family values. We often have conversations about raising our children in bilingual homes, whether we will baptize our children, and whether we will continue the tradition of the *quinceañera* (coming-of-age ceremony) when our daughters turn 15. Each cultural tradition that used to be taken for granted is reflected on and their implications are weighed. Comas-Diaz (2008) refers to this as the *multicultural brain* and "... entails the capacity to simultaneously hold multiple beliefs, shift from one viewpoint to another, integrate several cultural perspectives, and create a new reality out of divergent positions" (p. 16).

Voice and language continue to be the heart of our life journey. While Carmen continues to interpret for her mother when they are together in public, her mother now speaks enough English to get by when Carmen is not available. Most importantly, Carmen now knows her voice and can express her emotions and not feel self-indulging for doing so. This transformation began in college when she went to the counseling center and met a therapist that changed her life. Vasquez (2008) could have been describing Carmen's experience when she wrote,

> A Latina client who learned to withdraw into silence in the context of her family, because being outspoken was seen as a sign of disrespect and elicited punishment, may have a tendency to be hard on herself in the context of interactions which require verbal discussion, but which are intimidating. (p. 25)

This re-claiming of voice within a cultural context is not uncommon in my clinical work with Latinas. It isn't simply being more assertive about needs, but gaining a consciousness about the debilitating effects of *aguantando* (enduring) when it involves keeping silent and internalizing pain. A reformulation of *aguantando* to include power and movement forward is *sobrepasando* (exceeding/transcending) and involves knowing when silence is a choice rather than a mandate.

Carmen and I both struggle with language in different ways. Spanish is my second language, whereas it is the dominant language for Carmen. We both work to maintain linguistic proficiency, but experiences of linguistic prejudice (Carreira, 2000) abound. Dialects can been used as indicators of social class and education (Corvalán, 1994, as cited in Carreira, 2000), and in our experiences speaking Spanish was another social identity. A painful, yet important training experience for me was during my first year of graduate school when I worked at a community agency. As I was speaking with a woman on the telephone in Spanish, she commented with laughter and derision in her voice, "*Hablas como un Mexicana* (You talk like a Mexican)." I was dumbfounded by her comment on many levels and numerous thoughts raced through my head in a flash. I was surprised that she suddenly shifted to the informal form of "you" in that one comment, I noted the disdain in her voice and wondered if she disliked Mexicans, I was embarrassed that perhaps my Spanish wasn't good enough (internalized oppression), and I was angry by her rudeness. The only response I could think of in the moment was "Thank you;" but that one experience taught me that being "a blank slate" with my clients was not possible. Speaking Spanish with my clients invariably turned to personal questions about where I grew up and how I learned Spanish. I honored their questions, but also used this as a point of conversation about being bilingual, shame around language use and disuse, and experiences of linguistic prejudice.

As Carmen and I enter our forties as married, professional women with children, we laughingly embrace the contradictions in our lives. We help each other approach challenges and fears head on, and no longer feel the need to run past them in silence. We have the language to name injustice and oppression in our lives, and have the tools to initiate change. We also accept that our spiritual connection with each other and the divine surpasses language, but the best way to describe us are as *hermanas de corazón y alma* (sisters of the heart and soul).

REFERENCES

Aguirre, C., Bermúdez, J. M., Cardona, J. R. P., Zamora, J. A., & Reyes, N. A. (2005). The process of integrating lanauge, context, and meaning.: The voices of bilingual and bicultural therapists. In M. Rastogi & E. Wieling (Eds.), *Voices of Color: First-person Accounts of Ethnic Minority Therapists* (pp. 189–209). Thousand Oaks, CA: Sage.

Altarriba, J., & Santigo-Rivera, A. L. (1994). Current perspectives on using linguistic and cultural factors in counseling the Hispanic client. *Professional Psychology: Research and Practice, 25*, 388–397.

Anzaldúa, G. (1987). *Borderlands, la frontera: The new mestiza.* San Francisco: Aunt Lute Books.

Baumrind, D. (1966). Effects of authoritative parental control on child behavior. *Child Development, 37*, 887–907.

Bond, M. H., & Lai, T. M. (1986). Embarrassment and code-switching into a second language. *Journal of Social Psychology, 126*, 179–186.

Brown, L. S. (2010). *Feminist therapy.* Washington, DC: American Psychological Association.

Carreira, M. (2000). Validating and promoting Spanish in the United States: Lessons from linguistic science. *Bilingual Research Journal, 24*(4), 333–352.

Clauss, C. S. (1998). Language: The unspoken variable in psychotherapy practice. *Psychotherapy, 35*(2), 188–196.

Comas-Diaz, L. (2008). 2007 Carolyn Sherif award address: *Spirita*: Reclaiming womanist sacredness into feminism. *Psychology of Women Quarterly, 32*, 13–21.

Córdova, T. (1998). Power and knowledge: Colonialism in the academy. In C. Trujillo (Ed.), *Living Chicana theory* (pp. 17–45). Berkeley, CA: Third Woman Press.

Domenech Rodriguez, M. M., Donovick, M. R., & Crowley, S. L. (2009). Parenting styles in a cultural context: Observations of "protective parenting" in first-generation Latinos. *Family Process, 48*(2), 195–210.

Gonzalez, N. (2001). *I am my language: Discourses of women and children in the borderlands.* Tucson, AZ: The University of Arizona Press.

Maccoby, E. E., & Martin, J. A. (1983). Socialization within the context of the family: Parent-child interaction. In P. H. Mussen & E. M. Hetherington (Eds.), *Handbook of child psychology: Vol. 4 socialization, personality, and social development* (4th ed., pp. 1–101). New York: Wiley.

Montgomery, L. M. (1908). *Anne of green gables: Four books in one set complete and unabridged.* Retrieved December 29, 2011 from Kindle Books.

Morales, A., & Hanson, W. E. (2005). Language brokering: An integrative review of the literature. *Hispanic Journal of Behavioral Sciences, 27*, 471. DOI: 10.1177/0739986305281333

Neimann, Y. F. (2004). Stereotypes of Chicanas and Chicanos: Impact on family functioning, individual expectations, goals, and behaviors. In R. Velasquez, L. M. Arellano, B. McNeill (Eds.), *The Hadbook of Chicana/o psychology and mental health* (pp. 61–82). Mahwah, NJ: Lawrence Erlbaum Associates, Inc.

Orellana, M. F., Dorner, L., & Pulido, L. (2003). Accessing assets: Immigrant youth's work as family translators or "para-phrasers." *Social Problems, 50*(4), 505–524. DOI: 10.1525/sp.2003.50.4.505

Teish, L. (1996). The warrior queen: Encounters with a Latin lady. In A. Castillo (Ed.), *Goddess of the Americas/La Diosa de las Americas: Writings on the virgin of Guadalupe* (pp. 137–146). New York, NY: Riverhead Books.

Vasquez, M. J. T. (2002). Latinas. *Women & Therapy, 25*(2), 23–38.

Comadres: The Healing Power of a Female Bond

LILLIAN COMAS-DIAZ
Transcultural Mental Health Institute, Washington, DC

The author discusses the use of comadre *therapy in feminist psychotherapy. Within the Latino culture a* comadre *is the relationship between the mother and her child's godmother. Literally meaning co-mother, a* comadre *is special bond between women who are intimate friends. A clinical case is provided to illustrate the use of comadre therapy.*

INTRODUCTION

In this article I discuss the effect of a sisterhood bond on my healing journey. I explore the nurturing effect of this relationship on my development as a psychotherapist. In this vein, I present how *mujerismo* (Latina feminism) cultivated my commitment to feminist therapy. As a result, I present the concept of *comadre* (co-mother) to designate feminist psychotherapy within a *mujerista* perspective. Finally, I discuss how I conduct psychotherapy through a *mujerista* empowerment orientation. A case vignette illustrates this approach.

FAMILISM: A COLLECTIVE CONNECTION

"Are we so close because we're cousin sisters?"

–Lillian

"No, we have been close since the beginning of time."

–Elba

A relational value, familism highlights the relevance of family relationships. In this fashion, familism underscores the cultural connectors present among Latinos. As a result, many Latinos refer to themselves as members of *la gran familia* because familism extends to biological as well as non-biologically related individuals. One vivid example is the concept of *hijos de crianza*. A collectivistic notion, *hijos de crianza* refers to individuals who receive parental care and nurture, but are not legally adopted by their families. This conception illustrates the permeability of Latino boundaries because *hijos de crianza* may or may not be biologically related to their families. Consonant with this perception, my cousin Elba and I became *hermanas* (sisters) *de crianza*. We lived in the same house—Elba—upstairs with her parents and brother, and I—downstairs, with my maternal grandparents.

Born in Chicago, I spent my first six years in a frigid land before moving to the fiery Caribbean. I arrived to my maternal grandparents' home after a major hurricane devastated the town. To cope with such a crisis the town people resorted to familism. As an outsider, however, I had not directly experienced the natural disaster. Nonetheless, familism designated me as an insider because I was present during the recovery from the storm. In this fashion, traumatized classmates welcomed me as a member of their familia.

"Talk to Lillian," Elba told the distressed children, and as a result, they were drawn to my empathic witnessing. This incident signaled the life long support that my sister of the heart offered to me as an emerging therapist. Certainly, Elba nurtured a healing gift. She saw in me what I could not perceive. Thanks to her encouragement I began to see myself as a helper.

Once more, familism facilitated this process. Latino familism assigns females the helping roles of nurturers, healers, educators, and diviners. One vivid example—the role of folk healer affords females independence at multiple levels—personal, financial, and social (Koss-Choinino, 1992). The women in my family embodied these helping roles. For instance, my maternal grandmother worked as a cook, my aunt Paulina was a teacher, my mother was a nurse, and my paternal grandmother earned her living as a psychic. All of these women expected me to become a nurse, just like my mother. However, at a young age I knew that I wanted to be a different kind of a helper. After my experience with the recovery from the storm, I decided to become a psychotherapist (Comas-Diaz, 2011). In retrospect, I see that a psychotherapist is a combination of all the female helper roles. Moreover, when I announced that was to become a clinical psychologist, Elba replied: "You can fly if you want to."

WOMANHOOD: MARIANISMO AND MUJERISMO

As sisters of the heart, we promised to become each other's *comadre* (co-mother). The term *comadre* describes the relationship between the mother and the godmother of a child. The *comadre* relationship strengthens the special bond between women who are intimate friends. Such co-parenting system originates when the child is baptized. Literally meaning co-mother, the *comadre* bond is culturally anchored in familism. Therefore, becoming each other's *comadre* was a logical developmental phase in our sisterly bond.

Adolescence, however, threatened our intimate bond. Our two-year age difference seemed to grow decades. Elba surrounded herself with her peers, and I felt ostracized. Moreover, a female cultural milestone accentuated the disparity. Elba's *quinceañera* (sweet 15) was a formal party where she danced waltz with her father, relatives, and friends. A *quinceañera* is a ceremony that celebrates the transition from girlhood to young womanhood. Such tradition announces the female coming of age by "presenting" the young woman to the community, signaling that she is of marriageable age (Palfrey, 1997). Since I knew that I was not going to have a *quinceañera* party, I struggled with ambivalence. On one hand, I vicariously enjoyed Elba's *quinceañera*. The mesmerizing ritual nourished my young romanticism. On the other hand, I was proud of my parents' critical thinking. "Quinceañera is an elitist pretension," my parents declared. Indeed, my parents—who lived in Chicago for a decade, and later returned to Puerto Rico–refused to succumb to sociocultural conventions. Instead, I settled for a different kind of celebration.

When I turned 15 my maternal grandmother promised to cook my favorite dish—*arroz con gandules* (rice with pigeon peas). As we shelled the *gandules* (pigeon peas), Abuela told me a family story. Her beautiful 15-year-old sister Maria had fallen in love with Carlos. Due to her parents' strictness, Maria and Carlos began to date secretly. When my great-grandparents found out about the romance, they forbade Maria from seeing Carlos. "Papa was very rigid," Abuela explained. "On a sunny afternoon," Abuela continued," Maria and I were shelling *gandules* in our house balcony, just like you and I are doing now. Carlos suddenly appeared out of nowhere. He pulled out a gun, shot Maria dead, and then killed himself."

My grandmother became silent after a tear fell on the bowl of *gandules*. She wiped another tear from her left cheek before she continued: "I don't remember what happened afterwards. I only remember the *gandules* full of blood. " Abuela continued wiping her tears. After a long silence she said:

> "I promised to let my children choose."
> "What do you mean?"
> "That's how your mother married a Black man," Abuela said.

Abuela grew up in a marianista society. A traditional Latino gender role, marianismo (from Maria) expects women to emulate the Virgin Mary (Virgen Maria). Therefore, marianismo entails the veneration of female virginal purity, moral and spiritual superiority over men, and selfless motherhood. In other words, marianismo reveres chastity, other-directedness, self-sacrifice, and duty. According to Stevens (1973), marianista women are expected to be modest, compliant, and unassertive. Marianismo is a Latino sociohistorically situated concept. In their book, *The Maria Paradox*, psychotherapists Rosa M. Gil and Carmen I. Vasquez (1996) affirmed that marianismo provided women with respect and protection within traditional societies, but "in today's North America, marianismo is the invisible joke that binds capable, intelligent, ambitious Latinas" (p. 7).

Abuela was a marianista by birth and a mujerista by choice. Like marianismo, mujerismo highlights the centrality of females in Latino life. However, different from marianistas, mujeristas are womanists, or Alice Walker's (1983) coined term for women-of-color feminists. Following this analysis, mujeristas, address the role of racism, neocolonialism, and imperialism in gender relations. From the Spanish word *mujer*, meaning woman, mujerismo is Latina feminism. Consequently, mujeristas identify their marginalization from the White feminism, Latino patriarchy, cultural imperialism, dominant society's oppression, neo colonialism, and economic domination as precipitants of their psychopolitical birth (Comas-Diaz, 2008a). Mujerismo responds to the needs of Latinas in the United States. It helps them to foster transculturation or the emergence of a new culture out of two different ones, in order to resist assimilation (Comas-Diaz, 2008a). Moreover, mujerismo helps Latinas to interpret cultural differences as a source of power.

Like their womanist sisters, mujeristas honor the Spirit. Mujeristas ground their spirituality in a gender specific and cultural context. For example, Latino folk spirituality and popular religion have indigenous roots that pay tribute to a feminine divinity. To illustrate, many Catholic Latino(a)s tend to identify more with the Virgin Mary than with Jesus. Moreover, in most Latin American Catholic churches the figure of the Virgin Mary is situated in a prominent place, many times, above the figure of Jesus (Tree, 2001). Mujeristas adhere to this popular spirituality. However, instead of emulating the Virgin Mary's Madonna purity, many mujeristas identity with la Virgen de Guadalupe's subversive and liberation role (Randall, 1996). As a syncretistic icon, Guadalupe is a Black Madonna warrior and a freedom fighter (Teish, 1996). The mother of the oppressed, la Virgen de Guadalupe imparts resilience to Latinas and energizes them to resist domination. Indeed, liberators carried her image as a banner of the Mexican revolution (Castillo, 1996).

As conceived by Ada Isasi-Diaz (1994), mujerista theology is anchored in the Latin American theology of liberation. Following this orientation, a central mujerismo element is the representation of everyday Latina. In other words, mujeristas side with Latinas who are non-White, poor, and oppressed. In this fashion, mujeristas honor the mixing of the races. Succinctly put, mujeristas recognize *mestizaje* (the mixing of European and indigenous people) and *mulataje* (the mixing of Europeans with Africans, and other races) as means to struggle against imperialism, oppression, and neocolonization.

In reality, mestizaje and mulataje constitute subversive positions against the idealized Eurocentric model (Buscaglia-Salgado, 2003). Certainly, mestizo(a)s and mulatto(as) racially represent the majority of the Latino population. In this way, a brown, poor, female Guadalupe is the mestiza daughter of the Spaniard (from Extremadura) Santa Maria de Guadalupe and the Aztec goddess Tonantzin (Castillo, 1996). The Creole Guadalupe is a mujerista icon that responds to the realities of mixed race Latinas by empowering them to combat and overcome oppression.

A mujerista, my grandmother was devoted to the Virgin de Monserrate, the black Madonna from Puerto Rico. Additionally, she prayed to Saint Martin de Porres, the Peruvian mulatto who is the patron saint of mixed race people. Abuela's dedication to these spiritual figures taught me to honor myself as a mixed race female. Moreover, her cuentos (stories) carried the commandments of mujerismo:

The Ten Commandments of My Abuela's Mujerismo

Honor your inner divinity.
Ask for help—She will respond.
Be aware of who you are, but be open to change.
Remember that your identity transcends your self.
Aim to empower others.
Encourage connectedness and solidarity.
Fight oppression.
Become resilient and learn to overcome adversity.
Transform low self-esteem into self-love.
Dance with life, when the music changes, choreograph new steps.

CIVIL RIGHTS AND WOMEN'S MOVEMENT

Elba and I recovered from our adolescent fracture as we roomed together while studying at the University of Puerto Rico. Besides sharing books and dreams, we exchanged bliss and sadness. Although we consoled each other's broken hearts; politics became our shared mission. We witness the Civil Rights and Women's movements as they stormed the island. We championed the rights of the disenfranchised. Black Power also reached Puerto Rico, albeit with difficulty, because internalized collective racism pities sibling against sibling. During this period I began to self identify as Black by wearing an Afro hairdo. Unfortunately, my gendered racial affirmation exiled me from my family. "Why do you want to look like a jabá?" my mulatto father demanded. Jabá is a pejorative term used to describe a mixed race woman with high yellow skin and kinky hair. As I refused to torture my "bad" hair and scalp with irritant hair creams, my father stopped speaking to me. Elba was the only family member who supported my gendered racial manifesto.

The luminescence of her blond, "good" hair, amber colored eyes, and porcelain doll complexion matched the passion of her solidarity. As I began to sit in the "Black " area of the university cafeteria, Elba accompanied me by sitting besides me. She seemed to ignore the "you don't belong" stares from my racial siblings. Without a doubt, Elba's love sustained my developing racial pride in the midst of racism and sexist racism.

Like the Civil Rights, the Women's liberation movement arrived to the island. However, such feminist movement only addressed the needs of upper- and middle-class "White" women, dismissing the realities of poor, brown, and Black women. Ignorant of the realities of working class colored women, United States feminist voices were silenced by Puerto Rican liberation cries.

It is not surprising that Elba and I became activists. During our university years we attended political rallies, raised money for liberal causes, engaged in sociopolitical activities, and did community work. Moreover, we supported liberation movements. Pro Puerto Rican independence politics additionally anchored our sisterly connection. An anecdote illustrates such bonding.

One day I was marching with thousands of students peacefully in the university grounds. All of the sudden, policemen appeared from nowhere—their violent demeanor against the peaceful march. Under beautiful blue skies and a warm Caribbean sun, I watched in terror a policeman hitting his club a pregnant student's belly. I froze. Club in hand, the policeman ran towards me. Out of nowhere, I felt a pull that forced me to run. "I knew you needed me," Elba said as we ran away from the policeman.

Our connection seemed to be genetic since our maternal great grandmothers had psychic gifts. A family anecdote asserted that upon her death, one of our great grandmothers "visited" the other. Belief in farewell visitations after death are common occurrence among many Latinos (Comas-Diaz, 2006). After hearing this anecdote Elba and I promised to follow our great grandmothers' example. We became interested in the metaphysical and supernatural. We visited folk healers. Here is another story.

Distressed after the breakup of a romantic relationship, I decided to consult a psychic. After the consultation I told Elba about the medium's vision. However, I was frustrated because the psychic's prophecies did not apply to me. "She is a charlatan," I concluded.

> "She is not," Elba said in a low voice. "Her prophecies were not about you," she added. "The were about me."
> "I see," I said. "The medium mentioned that I have a spiritual twin."

Latino spirituality informs this anecdote. Regardless of religiosity, most Latinos have an awareness of their spiritual ancestry (Comas-Diaz, 2006). For example, Latino spiritual beliefs are anchored in animism—the belief that everything (humans and non-humans alike) has a spirit (De La Cancela & Zavala Martinez, 1983). Such spirits interfere in people's lives through dreams, visions, intuitions, and other supernatural occurrences. Indeed, many Latinos do not end their relationship with their loved ones when they die (Council of National Psychological Associations, 2003) and thus, continue interacting with the deceased via supernatural means. Notably, a survey conducted by the Pew Hispanic Center and Pew Forum on Religion and Public Life (2007) found that many Latinos reported familiarity with supernatural experiences. Indeed, Latino spiritual and supernatural knowledge is transmitted through cultural osmosis.

Along with this analysis, Latino psychospirituality encourages the use of cultural beliefs for healing and spiritual development. Latinos' use of psychospirituality as a coping mechanism in the United States is consistent with the concept of ideological ethnicity. According to Alan Harwood (1981), the "ideological ethnicity" is a tendency to find meaning in life by revisiting cultural beliefs and rituals. Within this context, psychospirituality helps Latinos to intensify their sense of significance and purpose in life (Muñoz & Mendelson, 2005). To illustrate, many Latinos invoke the divinity multiple times in their daily life (Koss-Chioino & Vargas, 1999).

This is how Elba and I deepened our interest in psychospirituality. First, we honored our family history. Then, we subscribed to transpersonality or the belief that individual identity extends beyond the personal to include a collective definition of the self (Scotton, 1996). Afterwards, we added transrational methods to our study. Finally, we embraced holistic healing. For example, we studied yoga and contemplative disciplines. Having Elba as a fellow traveler enhanced my psychospiritual journey. This journey provided me with healing tools that I use today in my psychotherapeutic practice. To illustrate, I employ holistic mind–body techniques such as guided imagery creative visualization, meditation, mindfulness, focusing, and other mind–body approaches.

Becoming the Other

After completing college, I returned to the continental United States to become a psychologist. My parents encouraged my migration since they had left the island in their early adulthood. "Come with me," I asked Elba. She did not join me, instead, she gave me a farewell gift—a statue of a patient laying on a couch and a clinician sitting near taking notes.

Back in the United States I developed a profound nostalgia. Brazilians call it *saudade*, a homesickness that eats up your heart. Such cultural transition was Dantean—I stayed in Inferno for a long time. During this period I became the *other*. Racism, sexism and xenophobia were my custodians in my birth country. Trying to satisfy a spiritual hunger, I gratified myself with food. As a result, I turned into a woman I did not recognize in the mirror.

Eventually, I moved into purgatory. I learned English, survived gendered racism, lost weight, and reclaimed myself. Moreover, I obtained a doctorate in clinical psychology. Furthermore, I married Fred, a neuropsychopharmacologist who lived in Brazil as an adolescent. Elba also got married. We did not attend each other's wedding.

Elba gave birth to Gabriel and Laura. Unfortunately , she forgot our promise. Elba did not ask me to become her *comadre*. Her amnesia aggravated my otherhood condition. Paradoxically, otherhood helped to chisel my identity as a woman and as a psychotherapist. Like an alchemist, I worked to transform my pain into self-determination. With a new resilience I translated otherhood into multicultural psychology, and mujerismo into feminist psychotherapy. Moreover, syncretism helped me to marry multiculturalism with feminism. A syncretistic consciousness allowed me to connect womanism, mujerismo , and feminism (Comas-Diaz, 2008a). Under a mujerista rubric I trained Latinas to become culturally assertive (Comas-Diaz & Duncan, 1985). Along these lines, I fostered women's empowerment and liberation. Moreover, I helped women to awaken their inner sacred feminine (Comas-Diaz, 2008b),

As I engaged in a mujerista journey, I continued my transformation. This process led to reclaim my sister of the heart. My letters to Elba became short stories. Initially, I longed for what we had. However, a different aspect of the bond emerged. My *saudade* gave birth to generativity. In other words, as I reconnected with our sisterly bond, I began to mentor Elba's offspring. In particular, I mentored Laura, who later showed interest in becoming a healer. I reclaimed the promise to be a *comadre*.

Comadre Feminist Therapy

Midwife is another translation for the term *comadre*. Within this context, I see the feminist psychotherapist as the *comadre* (midwife) who helps clients give birth to themselves (Comas-Diaz, 2006). A *comadre* is your best friend—the person you call for help in the middle of the night. A *comadre* acts as a lay psychotherapist. She is an empowering healer. In her online article, *My Comadre, My Compass*, psychotherapist Lucia Lopez Plunkett stated that her *comadre* sees her as she is and allows her the space to express her feelings. Specifically, Dr. Lopez Plunkett stated that her *comadre*: "... helped me to gain confidence in my cultural identity, simply by loving herself enough to "be." Because of her, speaking in Spanish sounded beautiful and confident. When we are together, our energy is magnetic. The time endless. The world slows down and anything is possible" (http://tikitikiblog.com/my-comadre-my-compass/#axzz1O7PhnoOW).

In my experience, a feminist therapist of color can subscribe to a *comadre* orientation. In other words, a *comadre* therapist helps her clients to affirm their gendered cultural identity. Moreover, she fosters her clients' use of their female gifts of power, such as ethnogender intuition, prophetic abilities, and healing capacities.

Furthermore, a *comadre* therapist acts as a liberation practitioner. Without a doubt, a comadre helps women to empower themselves. She helps women to build their strengths, reclaim their voice, and develop resilience against adversity. Likewise, a *comadre* therapist engages in activism. Within her activist role, a *comadre* fosters liberation by promoting critical consciousness of oppressive realities. Even more, a *comadre* therapist helps clients to awake their inner freedom fighter. As an example, a group of female activists has taken the name Comadres to mobilize their efforts. The Comite de Madres Monsignor Romero (Comadres) is an activist organization whose mission is to aid victims and families of the Civil War in El Salvador (http://www.comadres.org/main_english.html).

Along these lines, a comadre therapist promotes action for personal and social transformation. She uses cultural and gender specific resources to enhance this process. Furthermore, a comadre therapist promotes decolonization. She helps women to reduce their colonial mentality, deconstruct their internalized oppression, and reclaim their ethnocultural selves. Consider the following case vignette.

Linda Remembers Who She Is

Linda, a 37-year-old widow with two children, ages 8 (son) and 6 (daughter), came to see me after her sister Carla referred her to a therapist. An editor in a publishing house, Linda had worked at the same organization for the last 10 years. She was the youngest daughter of a Mexican woman teacher and an Afro Peruvian male engineer. As a result, Linda self identified as a *morena*—a mixed-race woman.

Julio, Linda's husband, had died in a car accident the previous year. Linda experienced a complicated bereavement reaction to Julio's death. Specifically, she had sleeping problems, anxiety while driving, depressed mood, and irritability.

After Julio's death, Carla, who was divorced and without children, moved with Linda. She contacted the servidor system in order to help Linda with her children. Like an extended family, the servidor system includes Latinos who use their influential positions to serve community members in need. Since Julio was an active member of the Latino community, the servidores quickly responded to Carla's request for help. Moreover, as Linda and Carla were raised Catholic, they began attending church. The priest recommended Linda to see a nun for grief counseling. Linda abruptly ended the counseling without giving an explanation.

A self-reliant woman, Linda acknowledged difficulty in asking and receiving help. Indeed, Carla had referred Linda to therapy due to frequent arguments about housework. Establishing rapport with Linda was difficult.

Her level of irritability interfered with the development of a therapeutic alliance. Nonetheless, there was a turning point in the emergence of the therapeutic relationship. Linda saw a book—"*I Know Just What you Mean: The Power of Friendship in Women's Lives*"—on my desk. " I love that book," she said. The book seemed to trigger a memory of a lost intimate friend.

Although Linda was born in the United States, her family moved to Mexico when she was four years old. She completed her primary school in Mexico City, where she met her best friend Lupe. "We were like twins, " Linda observed, "Eventhough we were the opposite of each other in the color spectrum." While discussing her friendship with Lupe, Linda stated that her Mexican classmates ostracized her due to her dark skin and African features. "Carla did not have that problem, because she looks White," Linda said.

> "How was that for you?" I asked.
> "My classmates called me *negra fea*, that's how it was," Linda said in a loud voice.
> "How did you feel about being called ugly Black?"
> "Lupe used to say that I was like my name, *linda* (pretty)."
> "What happened to Lupe?
> "I don't know ... We lost contact after we left Mexico."

After this session, Linda began to dream about Mexico. We interpreted her dreams both from a mainstream psychotherapy perspective as well as from a cultural orientation. Linda then related a dream she had the night before Julio's death. In her dream Linda saw Coatlicue, the Aztec goddess of death, who invited her to dance. "I talked to no one about it," she said. Linda interpreted the dream as a premonition of Julio's death. "I could have warned him," she explained. "This is why I feel responsible for Julio's death."

I explored Linda's psychodynamics around her marriage and Julio's death. Although she reported having a positive relationship with her husband, we worked on her grief. Additionally, I helped Linda to release repressed emotions through holistic experiential approaches. We first worked with relaxation and desensitization. Then, I suggested a Buddhist meditation to release guilt. Linda found these approaches useful. After she became centered, we analyzed her Coatlicue dream following a psychospiritual approach. As the goddess of life and death, Coatlicue is also known as the mother of the gods. Within this framework we worked on reframing Linda's interpretation. Through a guided imagery Linda released her negative interpretation. She then connected Coatlicue's motherhood aspect with her own motherhood as a widow. In other words, Linda reinterpreted her sense of responsibility for Julio's death and translated it into her responsibility towards her children. This reframing provided Linda with an enhanced meaning in life.

Feeling lighter from her guilt, Linda expressed a desire to explore her Mexican childhood chapter. As a result, we examined her intimate friendship with Lupe. During this exploration Linda connected her daughter's age (6 years) with her own age when she left Mexico. Realizing the significance of her daughter's age at the time of losing Julio, Linda understood her complicated bereavement as a reaction to her multiple ungrieved losses. Longing to reconnect with her lost best friend, Linda used social media (Facebook) to look for Lupe. She was pleasantly surprised to find out that Lupe was living in her same city. Linda and Lupe reunited after 31 years. Needless to say, the reconnection was healing for both women.

Linda and Lupe renewed their intimate friendship. Having shared a passion for reading, Linda invited Lupe to join *Reading with Las Comadres* (http://www.lascomadres.org/lco/lco-eng/index.html). *Las Comadres para las Americas* (http://www.lascomadres.org/) sponsor this international book club that specializes in Latina authors (Jordan, 2007). *Las Comadres para las Americas* is a networking group that highlights the relevance of female friendship s among Latinas under the comadres concept.

Linda remained in therapy for two years. During this time she grieved multiple losses. Linda's symptoms decreased and her relationship with her sister Carla improved. Likewise, our therapeutic relationship progressed throughout the diverse stages of therapy. As I previously stated, Linda's initial resistance to therapy was an obstacle at the beginning of treatment. After her depressive symptoms subsided in response to holistic and cognitive behavioral therapy, Linda began to trust me as her clinician. Around this time, Lupe gave Linda a gift—a Virgin of Guadalupe medallion. Linda became inseparable from her medallion.

> "I need to work on accepting myself as I am," Linda said. "Can you help me remember who I am?"

In response to Linda's question, I treated her with a feminist therapy with cultural and gender specific elements. This approach aimed to solidify her racial gender identity. During this process we, examined her role in the family as the darkest daughter. I used a mujerista feminist therapy approach to address Linda's gender and racial pain. To illustrate, the use of critical consciousness (Freire, 1973) helped to address Linda's internalized sexist racism. Moreover, ethnocultural transference and countertransference (Comas-Diaz & Jacobsen, 1991) facilitated the unfolding of the healing process. Initially Linda developed a transference towards me similar to her relationship with her sister Carla. Perhaps my "expert" role as a Latina therapist promoted such transferential reaction. Consequently, I monitored Linda's ethnocultural transference of ambivalence towards me. As our therapeutic relationship evolved, a mirroring transference emerged. In other words, Linda identified with me as a mixed race Latina. "We could be sisters," she told me.

Given the similarities between us, such as being mixed race Latinas, a history of (im)migration and transculturation, a resultant need to remember ourselves, experiencing the loss of a sister of the heart, among others; I carefully monitored my ethnocultural countransference. To achieve this goal, I saw a consultant.

After Linda strengthened her trust in me, we cemented the therapeutic relationship. At this point I helped Linda to identify her negative self-schema. Most of her negative schema was related to her racial identity and her displaced anger and irritability towards significant others. We then engaged in challenging and reframing such schema. We completed the process when Linda reprocessed the negative schema and incorporated positive self-identifications as a morena (dark skin Latina). To complement this work, Linda began reading memoirs of mixed race women. During our final therapy session Linda presented me with her unpublished book, *Remembering Who I Am.*

Reflection

As a feminist psychotherapist, I believe in fostering women's support systems. In most cases my clients' support has consisted of female intimate friends. Throughout this experience, the comadre system has taught me lessons that I incorporate into my feminist psychotherapy. Interestingly, most these lessons are a psychological translation of my grandmother's mujerista advice:

Ten comadre lessons
Witness women's pain and joy
Assist women in giving birth to themselves
Recognize women's cultural groundedness
Cultivate women's gifts of power
Promote women's awakening, empowerment, and liberation
Heal with a thinking heart
Mentor others and mentor yourself
Assist women in choreographing their dance of life
Nurture women's connection to their inner sacredness
Foster female bonding—support sister of the heart relationship

CONCLUSION

As life went on, a series of adversities visited my sister of the heart. First, Elba's husband left her for another woman. Then, she lost her job. Afterwards, Elba's father died, her mother became demented, and eventually died. Life had more in store. Elba was diagnosed with breast cancer. She battled the illness with courageous spirit. She went from walking with a cane, to using a wheelchair, to not being able to leave her bed. And ...

That was years ago. Currently, two pieces bookmark my days. The first one is a statue that adorns my psychotherapy office. This figure depicts a patient laying on a couch and a clinician sitting near taking notes. The statue infuses my psychotherapist role with *comadre* energy. The second bookmark is at my home. From my living room I admire a cherry blossom tree that we planted on the front yard in memory of Elba's life. This tree is a living proof of my enduring connection to the sister of my heart.

REFERENCES

Buscaglia-Salgado, J. F. (2003). *Undoing Empire: Race and nation in the Mulatto Caribbean*. Minneapolis: University of Minnesota Press.

Castillo, A. (Ed.). (1996). *Goddess of the Americas/La Diosa de las Americas: Writings on the Virgin of Guadalupe* (pp. 137–146). New York: Riverhead Books.

Comadres, Las. Retrieved on July 18, 2007 from. http://www.lascomadres.org/).

Comas-Diaz, L. (2006). Latino healing: The integration of ethnic psychology into psychotherapy. *Psychotherapy. Theory, Research, Practice & Training, 43*(4), 43–6453.

Comas-Diaz, L. (2008a). *Spirita*: Reclaiming womanist sacredness in feminism. *Psychology of Women Quarterly, 32*, 13–21.

Comas-Diaz, L. (2008b). Our inner Black Madonna: Reclaiming sexuality, embodying sacredness. *Women & Therapy, 31*(1), 5–20.

Comas-Diaz, L. (2011). Transcultural woman: Healing in a strange land. In L. Comas-Diaz & M. B. Weiner (Eds.), *Women psychotherapists: Journeys in healing*. New York: Jason Aronson.

Comas-Diaz, L., & Duncan, J. W. (1985). The cultural context: A factor in assertiveness training with mainland Puerto Rican women. *Psychology of Women Quarterly, 9*(4), 46-3475.

Comas-Díaz, L., & Jacobsen, F. M. (1991). Ethnocultural transference and countertransference in the therapeutic dyad. *American Journal of Orthopsychiatry, 61*(3), 392–402.

Council of National Psychological Associations (2003, November). *Psychological treatment of ethnic Minority Populations*. Washington, DC: the Association of Black Psychologists.

De La Cancela, V., & Zavala Martinez, I. (1983). An analysis of culturalism in Latino mental health: Folk medicine as a case in point. *Hispanic Journal of Behavioral Sciences, 5*(3), 251–274.

Freire, P. (1973*). Education for critical consciousness*. New York: Seabury.

Gil, R. M., & Vasquez, C. I. (1996). *The Maria paradox: How Latinas can merge old world traditions with new world self-esteem*. New York: Putnam.

Harwood, A. (1981). *Ethnicity and medical care*. Cambridge, MA: Harvard University.

Isasi-Diaz, A. M. (1996). *Mujerista theology: A theology for the twenty-first century.* Maryknoll, NY: Orbis.

Jordan, T. (2007, September 5). Reading with Las Comadres will highlight Latinas authors. Available from www.publishers.org/main/PressCenter/LasComadres Release.htm

Koss-Chioino, J. D. (1992). *Women as healers, women as patients: Mental health care and traditional healing in Puerto Rico*. Boulder, CO: Westview Press.

Muñoz, R. F., & Mendelson, T. (2005). Toward evidence-based interventions for diverse populations: The San Francisco general hospital prevention and treatment manuals. *Journal of Clinical and Consulting Psychology, 73*(5), 790–799.

Palfry, D. H. (1997). La Quinceañera: A celebration of budding womanhood. Retrieved on March 11, 2011 from http://www.mexconnect.com/articles/3192-la-quincea%C3%B1era-a-celebration-of-budding-womanhood

Pew Hispanic Center and Pew Forum on Religion & Public Life (2007, April 25). Pew Research Center. Washington, DC. Available from www.pewhispanic.org

Randall, M. (1996). Guadalupe, subversive Virgin. In Ana Castillo (Ed.), *La Diosa de las Américas (Goddess of the Americas): Writings on the Virgin of Guadalupe* (pp. 113–123). New York: Riverhead Books.

Scotton, B. W. (1996). Introduction and definition of transpersonal psychiatry. In B. W. Scotton, A. B. Chinen, & John R. Battista (Eds.), *Textbook of transpersonal psychiatry and psychology* (pp. 3–8). New York: Basic Books.

Stevens E. P. (1973). Marianismo: The other face of machismo in Latin America. In A. Pescatelo (Ed.), *Female and male in Latin America.* Pittsburgh: University of Pittsburgh Press.

Teish, L. (1996). The warrior queen: Encounters with a Latin lady. In A. Castillo (Ed.), *Goddess of the Americas/La Diosa de las Americas: Writings on the Virgin of Guadalupe* (pp. 137–146). New York: Riverhead Books.

Tree, I. (2001). *Sliced iguana: Travels in Mexico.* New York: Penguin Books.

Walker, A. (1983). *In search of our mothers' garden: Womanist prose.* New York: Harcourt Brace Jovanovich.

A Complicated Friendship

LOUISE BORDEAUX SILVERSTEIN
Ferkauf Graduate School of Psychology, Yeshiva University, Bronx, New York

The author presents a complicated friendship with a woman who helped to raise her children. As a feminist therapist, the author is aware of the non-egalitarian nature of an employer/employee relationship, resulting in a complicated friendship. She discusses the valuable lessons she learned from her comadre (co-mother or allomother) on poverty, Latino culture, and immigration. The author applies these valuable lessons to her work as a feminist therapist, supervisor, and teacher.

Ever since Connie Blumenthal and I discovered the joys of roller-skating and hopscotch in elementary school, I've had very close female friends. In addition to providing companionship and intimacy, these friendships have functioned to decrease anxiety as I negotiated difficult life periods. Barbara, Marilyn, and I supported each other through graduate school. Susan was a life saving source of positive affirmation as I struggled to balance finishing my dissertation, full-time work, and the birth of my first child. Rachel helped me to maintain some degree of sanity during the years that I negotiated the challenges of raising young children and building my career. All of these women were sources of understanding and emotional comfort for me personally, and they also helped to stabilize my marriage. Without their friendship that nourished and supported me through the years, I might well have succumbed to the stresses and terminated my now 44-year marriage.

In this essay, I describe a friendship of almost 30 years with my *comadre*, Blanca Cienfuegos, who helped me raise my children and confront the challenges of balancing "babies and briefcases" in the context of a dual career marriage. This friendship is "complicated" because our relationship of employed/employer casts a shadow of unequal power over the authenticity and intimacy of our friendship. Blanca has worked for me for 27 years, and continues to work for me even now. Despite this complication, I want to honor the importance of this relationship in my life and hers. As I tell our story, I will address these complications.

I will discuss the lessons that my friendship with Blanca has taught me about poverty, Latino culture, and immigration. These lessons have improved my practice as a feminist therapist and supervisor, as well as a teacher of multiculturalism. These lessons illustrate how a feminist perspective toward marginalized women, uninformed by multicultural sensitivity and humility, can actually be disempowering. Finally, I will briefly address the importance of female coalitions in evolutionary theory.

OUR STORY

I first met Blanca when she did house cleaning for a friend. She seemed slightly younger than I, with dark curly hair and a big smile. I was impressed with her work ethic and her amazingly positive disposition. She had recently arrived from El Salvador and spoke no English. Although I did not speak Spanish, I spoke enough French to get a sense of her personality.

I decided to hire Blanca as a nanny when my second child, Jesse, was 8 months old. I knew that she was the oldest of 13 children, so I was confident that she could manage 7-year-old Eva and infant Jesse. I wanted both children to be bilingual, so I hired a Spanish tutor for Eva, an English tutor for Blanca, and I took an intensive course in Spanish. My husband, Barry, was on his own. I was working part-time in private practice, so my work hours were limited and flexible. Blanca and I proved to be a good team, sharing childcare and housework.

As I got to know Blanca better, I began to feel very close to her. At some point, I realized that she reminded me of my grandmother. I had a very unconflicted and loving relationship with my grandmother who took care of me when I was a small child. My grandmother was from Eastern Europe and spoke Yiddish and almost no English. She, like Blanca, courageously struggled to adjust to a culture very different from her own. I admired both women's indomitable spirits as they faced the hardships of leaving their countries, their families, everything that was familiar to them, in order to make a new life for themselves.

After several months of being together, I began to learn more about Blanca's life. El Salvador was in the middle of a civil war. Life was dangerous. Work was virtually non-existent. Blanca had come here with the help of a cousin, but she had two daughters of her own that she had to leave behind. This discovery threw me into an emotional tail- spin. How could I enjoy the privilege of Blanca taking care of my children while she missed her own? Barry and I decided to help Blanca bring her children to the U.S.

Blanca's children were close in age to mine. Tania was seven and Maricruz was four. They could not travel alone, so we arranged for Blanca's sister, Lola, to bring them. However, Lola did not feel that she could leave her own daughter, Guadalupe, so Lupe came with her. Thus began our adventure of living with Blanca, Lola and *las niñas*—five new family members.

At the time, we lived in a small three-bedroom apartment. I cannot even remember now where everyone slept. I know that it took four months for us to find an apartment for the Cienfuegos family. Each apartment they applied to refused to rent to them. Barry and I were going to guarantee the lease, so I could not understand what the problem was. Finally one of the prospective landlords told me that once "those people" moved in, large numbers of relatives moved in with them. Finally, after four months of failure, we decided to try a different strategy. I told a prospective landlord that Blanca was my sister-in-law—and that my brother, her husband, had been killed in the civil war. Perhaps the idea that her children were my nieces meant that they were not part of "those people" because the landlord agreed to allow them to rent the apartment.

From that point forward, we raised our children together. This arrangement came with benefits to all of us. Blanca was reunited with her children. My life stabilized because Blanca was not tempted to return to El Salvador. Blanca's children learned English more quickly; and my children became fluent in Spanish. Sadly, but importantly, as my children listened to Blanca's story, they learned what it meant to live in extreme poverty; to live in a country at war; to be an immigrant; and to be an illegal alien.

Although it may sound like our family did more of the giving, actually Blanca and I are even in the support we have given to each other. Many of the things that I did for Blanca were concrete. Over the years, we helped to bring many of Blanca's sisters and brothers to the U. S. We also helped Blanca get a green card, better housing, and after- school programs for the children. These things were important and changed the trajectory of her children's lives.

The things that Blanca has given me are intangible, but just as significant. She is an optimistic and loving person who treated my children with incredible generosity and love. I introduced Blanca as my children's second mother before I was aware of the term *comadre*. Her warmth and dependability freed me to have a fulfilling professional life unmarred by worry about leaving the children. Blanca's competence also allowed Barry and me to have time without the children. This was an absolutely essential component of our marriage. Like other friendships, Blanca was an important element in stabilizing our marriage.

Moreover, living with Blanca and her children also changed the trajectories of my children's lives. Both of them have profited from knowing

Spanish. Jesse chose to build a community center in Costa Rica when he was in high school, learning first hand what it is like to live in rural Latin America. Eva has lived in Spain and Argentina and was able to get her current job in Miami because of her fluency in Spanish. Both are committed to working for social justice. For example, Jesse began volunteering to work in the NYC AIDS walk when he was 13 years old, and has continued for the past 15 years. He now volunteers for the national organization that organizes these walks. Eva has always worked in the non-profit art world and is dedicated to making the arts accessible to low income children of color. After Hurricane Katrina, she took her dance company to New Orleans for two month-long residencies in New Orleans' oldest high school where she taught the children her repertory and led them in community dance performances. Experiencing the vicissitudes of Blanca's life as an immigrant, an uneducated household worker, and a single mother sensitized them to their privilege and inspired them to try to use it to help others.

Thus, Blanca and I have both provided opportunities to our children that would have been closed to them in the absence of our relationship. We also have given each other emotional support through many difficult times. I held her when her mother was sick and dying. Barry and I both helped her when she wanted to leave her boyfriend and was afraid that he would become violent. Blanca listened to my worries about the children, complaints about my husband, and frustrations with clients.

One of the most important gifts that Blanca gave me was to go with me twice a week for six years to visit my mother in the nursing home. I cannot express how important her companionship was to me during this difficult time. My mother and I had a very scratchy relationship. So, in addition to dealing with her cognitive deterioration and death, I was also trying to work out a better feeling about our life together.

Every Tuesday I would steel myself to make the visit. Blanca and I would stop for flowers and then walk the fifteen minutes to the nursing home. Blanca would be cheerful, talking about whatever was going on in her life, distracting me from the dread that I was feeling. When we got there, she would lovingly greet my mother and make small talk. Blanca can always find something to laugh about. So our time together would be upbeat and friendly. My mother was a master at "making the best of things." Blanca's mood would match my mother's and help me get through the visits. Blanca's company made them bearable for me.

Interestingly, I cannot remember any serious argument or angry confrontation between us. There have been minor skirmishes. Blanca was not a great disciplinarian—especially in terms of her beloved Jesse—and this often caused stress between us. At times I would come home to find Jesse doing something that I had asked Blanca not to let him do. When I asked Blanca why she was allowing it, she would reply: "I said 'no,' but he cried." Upsetting her cherished *niño* was not something Blanca could tolerate. Another area of frustration was Blanca's tendency to put things away. She was devoted to keeping the house neat and uncluttered, but she would neglect to tell us where she had decided things (e.g. car keys, eye glasses) should go. Although we would explain to her how frustrating this was—her behavior never changed. We just became reconciled to the fact that from time to time, things would be "Blanca-rized."

Despite the intimacy of our relationship, the fact that I was her employer cast a shadow over us. Over the years, our financial relationship has varied. When Jesse entered junior high school and I did not need full time help, I helped Blanca find other nanny jobs. However, she always continued to help me with housework one day a week. If her nanny job became part-time, she would work for me more than once a week until we could find another full time baby-sitting job. Baby-sitting is less physical, so she always preferred to spend more time in that kind of job. We have never been able to provide healthcare, but we share medical expenses with her. Several years ago, we gave her a lump sum payment as a pension.

These efforts do not change the power differential because Blanca still works for me. In earlier years, when she relied more on her work with me, she could never really get angry and threaten to walk away from the friendship as I could have done. At this point, Blanca has worked full time for another family for three years, and our contribution to her income is minimal. I am looking forward to the day that she moves to Florida to be closer to Tania (and Eva), so that our friendship will not be burdened by this financial issue. Until that time, we must negotiate the ambiguity of being both employed/employer and *hermanas del corazon.*

BLANCA AS PROFESSOR

Because my formal training in Spanish was so limited, I always referred to Blanca as *mi profesora de español.* She and *las niñas* taught me most of the Spanish that I know. This is not insignificant because being able to speak Spanish is virtually a necessity for my work in the Bronx. In addition to teaching me Spanish, Blanca taught me many life lessons that have improved my professional competence as a psychologist. As a White, upper middle class, highly educated member of an individualistic culture, understanding the subjective experiences of low income, under-educated, people of color from a collectivist culture has been a challenge. Yet these are the clients that I must train my students to work with in therapy. Having a personal relationship with Blanca and her family has helped me confront many stereotypes. Living with Blanca has tempered (but not eradicated completely – yet) my tendency to make critical judgments about people whose social context I do not understand. Most importantly, my relationship with Blanca has helped me develop humility in working with people from vastly different social locations.

One of the contexts in which I understood little about the reality of Blanca's life had to do with her reluctance to continue her education. Early on in our relationship, I wanted Blanca to get a GED so that she could get a job in a local hospital with health benefits. As a member of my U.S. Jewish culture, education has always been the road to social mobility. When we discussed this, she would always agree, but never enroll in ESL classes in our neighborhood community college. At first I was completely puzzled, and continually explained to her how much better her life and her children's lives would be with health insurance. After awhile, I realized that something important was interfering with her implementing this plan.

Because school was a place of safety and gratification for me, it was difficult to accept that Blanca was not going to do what I was sure was the "right thing" for her. As I took the time to ask for more details about her childhood, I learned that her position as oldest daughter meant that she had to leave school after fifth grade. I am still not sure exactly why Blanca has not gone back to school. She has never chosen to share her reasons with me. After learning about the responsibilities she shouldered as a child that made continuing in school impossible, I was more able to consider her subjective experience. I wondered whether she was ashamed at how limited her skills are, or if she had a traumatic event in school. Whatever the reason, her non-verbal behavior told me that this was a painful subject, and that returning to a structured educational setting was not an option for her. Although I was in the slow group for quite awhile, I now respect her decision.

Another topic which I had trouble accepting was Blanca's devotion to her mother. Blanca continuously sent home large sums of money. Her mother had 13 children. Her husband, Blanca's *pedrastro* (step-father), was reported to be a demanding, child abusing man. I could understand sending some money. However, my main feeling was "Keep your money to help *your* children. Your mother made her life decisions, now she has to live with them." For some period of time, I shared a version of these thoughts with Blanca. She just shook her head and said she wanted to help her mother. Over time, I came to understand the strength of *familism*. When family needs are great, members who have access to resources automatically share them. With this more nuanced understanding of collective values, I have been able to respond positively when Tania, the oldest sister of the oldest sister, bought her grandmother a home and functions as a bank for the entire extended family.

FEMINISM INFORMED BY MULTICULTURAL HUMILITY

I have written elsewhere of the dangers of White, heterosexual privilege (Silverstein & Brooks, 2010), with which I am only too familiar. As a White feminist therapist in the 1980s, I was multiculturally ignorant and arrogant. I had never had a professor of color in either undergraduate or graduate school. Although I majored in international relations as an undergraduate and learned a lot about other cultures and countries, the issue of how racism and colonialism constructed U.S. society had not been in the curriculum. Thus my feminism focused on deconstructing White male privilege, but never on White female privilege. Pewewardy (2004) has pointed out that when the concept, "the personal is political," relates only to the personal experiences of White middle class, heterosexual feminists, this perspective results in incomplete theories and practices that reinforce oppression. It was not until the middle 1990s when academic psychology finally began to consider racism that White feminism similarly began to move toward an intersectionalities perspective.

My education in this regard was facilitated by my membership in the American Psychological Association's Division 35, the Society for the Psychology of Women. This is one of two organizations (the American Family Therapy Academy is the other) that I have been a member of that has authentically acknowledged their own racism and became dedicated to social change. In addition to examining their own stereotypes and prejudices, the White members of Division 35 have made a conscious effort to share power with women of color. Thus I was able to meet women of color and White women who were dedicated to working toward an anti-racist stance. Some of these women became mentors and friends. I went to presentations and workshops that focused on integrating race, gender and class. So began my long journey toward multicultural competence and humility that is ongoing.

These academic experiences and relationships with professional women were essential. However, my personal relationship with Blanca was also essential because it presented me with opportunities to live the principles about which I was learning. These real life lessons forced me to step out of my narrow ethnocentrism and made me a better therapist, supervisor and teacher. The meta-lesson has been the realization that I must reserve judgment. I now realize that my subjective experiences are so different from many of the people that I work with, that making any kind of judgment from the perspective of my social location is inappropriate. Rather, as a therapist and supervisor, I must become an empathic qualitative researcher, trying to understand the social context and subjective experiences of "the other."

For example, one of my African-Caribbean female patients stayed for years with her drug-using, violent husband. Early in the therapy, before I had completely internalized how little I could really understand about someone from such a dramatically different social location, I could not understand why she stayed with him. She was the main breadwinner and assumed primary responsibility for childcare and housework. From my perspective, what was she getting from him? Over time, I was able to understand the importance of family stability to an African Caribbean woman whose parents had left her for many years to immigrate to the U.S.

Shortly after my client arrived in the U.S., her father left the family, and her mother remarried a violent man with several sons, one of whom sexually abused her. Although I had known all of this information at an intellectual level, I needed to reach a new place of empathic understanding of Blanca's life before I could emotionally integrate the reality of my client's life. I was then able to listen more patiently and with a positive valence to her ambivalence about leaving (see Silverstein [2004] for a discussion of this clinical case). Ultimately, she did leave when she was ready, and in her own way. Many years later, she lives happily with her new husband in Florida, close to her children and grandchildren. Accepting and ultimately respecting Blanca's decision not to return to a school was important in helping me understand how this client's history, so different from my own, made her behavior understandable.

Both my perspectives about Blanca's continuing her education and my initial impatience with my client's reluctance to leave her husband were well intentioned, but misguided attempts to empower women. These examples illustrate the danger of having a feminist perspective without multicultural humility. In both cases, I wanted these women to improve their lives. However, my lack of understanding of the parameters that constructed their lives could have resulted in their feeling disempowered. I wanted them to change in *my* way, and at *my* pace. This was impossible for them. If I had maintained that perspective, they might have felt like failures, weak rather than strong.

Another example illustrates how using an individualistic theoretical perspective uninformed by collectivist values risks harming, rather than helping families in conflict. I was recently visiting an externship site, observing a student work with a Latina family. The identified patient was the adolescent daughter in a single mother family. My student was encouraged by her supervisor to explain (lecture) to the mother that the daughter had to be relieved from childcare and allowed to spend more time with her friends. This separation-individuation perspective is a familiar one to those of us trained in the psychodynamic paradigm. However, it is totally blind to cultural differences.

After we returned to school, I spoke with the student, explaining that being a good daughter was a component of *familism* that was important to the mother, and also an essential element in the girl's identity development and positive sense of self. Thus, rather than dismissing the mother's expectations as toxic to her daughter's development, the therapist must first join with the mother and accept that her expectations were reasonable, within the context of her cultural frame. The therapist must also respect both the girl's longing to be a good daughter, and her desire to be with her friends. Moreover, the entire conflict should be normalized as a clash of cultural values, rather than a pathological mother-daughter conflict. Without this multicultural sensitivity, we would be engaging in mother-blaming and contributing to the daughter's difficulty finding a balance between her togetherness and individuality needs. Witnessing Blanca's need to take care of her mother and her extended family helped me achieve this empathic stance.

EVOLUTIONARY THEORY

This essay is a story of two working mothers. Since human primates evolved, from our foraging ancestors to contemporary women, mothers have "worked." Because human infants are born helpless and dependent on adults for an unusually long time, mothers have depended on others, alloparents, to help them raise their children.

Fathers can be active parents, although levels of paternal involvement within human social groups vary widely, ranging from caring to indifferent, and even total absence (Hewlett, 1992). Given this variability, Hrdy (1999) has argued that an exclusive focus on the importance of the mother-father bond to the survival of infants is not justified because, over the course of evolutionary history, infant survival would have been too vulnerable to paternal neglect, abandonment or even infanticide.

In contrast, Hrdy proposed that among early human primates other women, *allomothers*, provided alternative care to infants. She cited several examples of contemporary hunting-gathering cultures like the Efe pygmies in Central Africa, or residents of the Solomon Islands where women nurse each other's babies. Other examples in traditional societies include relatives who are adolescent girls, i.e., "prereproductives," and older postreproductive women, often grandmothers, who help to care for young children (Hrdy, 1999, p. 271).

In modern societies, many fathers are now much more involved in childcare than in previous generations. However, the most recent census figures indicate that mothers remain the primary caregiver in most U.S. families. In 2010, the U.S. Census Bureau reported that 15% of single parents were fathers (1.8 million), and estimated the number of stay-at-home dads at 154,000 out of the 25.3 million men who were part of married couples with children under 18 (U.S. Census Bureau, 2011). Where extended families are separated by distance or are otherwise unavailable, working parents must find additional caregivers, usually women, who are both qualified and willing. This now requires paying for allomothering.

Comadre can be translated as allomother, and that certainly is what Blanca has been in our family. However, she has not been simply a paid alternate caregiver. Rather, she has behaved as a member of our family, committed to the welfare of our children. Similarly, I have contributed to the wellbeing of her children. We have been *comadres* for each other. Our relationship, constructed by our shared need for help in raising our children, has generated a caring, and complicated friendship.

REFERENCES

Hewlett, B. (Ed.). (1992). *Father-child relations: Cultural and biosocial contexts.* New York: Aldine de Gruyter.

Hrdy, S. B. (1999). *Mother nature. A history of mothers, infants, and natural selection.* New York: Pantheon Books.

Pewewardy, N. (2004). The political is personal: The essential obligation of White feminist family therapists to deconstruct White privilege. *Journal of Feminist Family Therapy, 16,* 53–67.

Silverstein, L. B. (2004). Bowen family systems theory as feminist therapy. In M. Harway (Ed.), *Handbook of Couples Therapy* (pp. 103–118). New York: John Wiley & Sons.

Silverstein, L. B., & Brooks, G. (2010). Gender Issues in family therapy and couples counseling. In J. C. Chrisler & D. R. McCreary (Eds.), *Handbook of gender research in psychology.* New York: Springer-Verlag.

U.S. Census Bureau. (2011, June 19). Facts for features: Father's Day. www.census.gov/newsroom/releases/archives/ … /cb11-ff11.html

Sisters of the Heart Along the Way: The Power of the Female Mentoring Relationship

JENNIFER RUFF
University of California San Francisco, California Department of Corrections and Rehabilitation, San Francisco, California

Women's mentoring relationships with other women can have powerful effects on professional development and enrich the lives of both mentor and protégée. Women psychology students and early career psychologists are tasked with integrating their personal and professional identities and overcoming gender-related barriers to professional growth and career success. Mentors provide assistance negotiating these and other challenges to the junior professional's development. The author shares her experience as a woman student and early career psychologist in the context of her relationship with her woman mentor. She discusses her reconciliation of stereotyped beliefs about being a woman and a professional psychologist; processes significantly influenced by powerful characteristics of her mentoring relationship such as supportive encouragement, modeling, transparency, and spiritual connectedness. The author then explores the link between the relational qualities in the mentoring relationship and an enhanced overall approach to clinical work with patients. Last, the benefits of women's intimate relationships are discussed, followed by references that explore benefits and challenges, and models and strategies for women mentoring women. The author concludes that as a sister of the heart relationship, the mentoring bond between women can be a healing and empowering attachment.

As we left the room where we had our usual Friday group supervision, Dr. White turned to me and said, "You know, if you are intrigued by the idea of EMDR, come and see me in my private practice when you're finished here. There is so much more; things not always taught in settings like this." New to clinical practice as a graduate student, I was excited by my supervisor's offer. I watched her as she walked away, that familiar sense of curiosity about Kathryn White returning. Dr. White was a large woman who haphazardly wrapped herself in colorful flowing caftans, wore Birkenstocks year round, and always seemed slightly disheveled. She was as consistently soft spoken, sensitively attuned, and agile in accessing and applying a broad clinical knowledge base and skills. I wondered at what seemed to me at the time an odd mixture of traits and skill, as I tried to assimilate her image into my then existing mental representation of a professional psychologist. Where was the suit? The professional polish? Hers was a very different image than that of successful colleagues in my former career in corporate technology sales and service, and markedly different from the images that guided my expectations about professional psychologists.

However, not only would Kathryn and I continue our professional relationship, but our relationship would deepen and empower me both personally and professionally. We were to develop a strong connection and become true sisters of the heart; sisters even who would share a unique spiritual bond.

PATRIARCHY, WOMEN HEALERS, AND CLASSISM

The development of the images that guided my expectations of professionals in general and professional psychologists in particular, was influenced by several factors. Important influences were the patriarchal society in which I grew up and the aggrandizement and extension of stereotypical masculine traits in my childhood home.

In *Are All Women Healers?* Cushman (1991) noted, "today, the Western medical establishment reflects a historical legacy of discrimination" (p. 38). Certainly, university trained physicians have historically been white, male, and from economically advantaged backgrounds. In *Witches, Midwives, and Nurses: A History of Women Healers*, the authors (Ehrenreich & English, 1973) discussed the history of the suppression and even violent persecution of women healers by patriarchal societies. The oppressors sought to dominate Western medicine, and feared the empowerment of women in general, and their legitimization and potentially competitive position as healers. Authors describe the overt suppression of women healers as a political and class struggle, and that the pattern has risen and fallen with the status of women throughout history.

For hundreds of years, women's roles as healers were realized in serving the poor. They were scoffed at, illegalized, and even demonized. Ehrenreich

& English (1973) noted this trend in the witch burnings in Europe and the New World in which between 200,000 to 9,000,000 women were murdered; women who frequently were accused of sorcery for their participation in the healing of others. They quote the words of an English witch hunter "... we reckon all good witches, which do no hurt but good, which do not spoil and destroy, but save and deliver ... It were a thousand times better for the land if all Witches, but especially the blessing witch, might suffer death" (p. 44). They further note that it was believed that the work of the peasant wise-woman, or witch, interfered with the will of God, and that healing through her could only be achieved with the devil's assistance (p. 47). The trend continued centuries later in the outlawing of midwives in early twentieth-century America, who were mostly black or working class female immigrants, despite that university trained obstetricians at the time were found to be less competent (see Ehrenreich & English, 1973).

Messages from my early familial background fostered other misogynistic stereotypes. Levant (2011) noted that the socialization of traditional male gender roles predicted "... the devaluation of women, detachment from relationships, disdain of sexual minorities, neglect of health needs and violence." Messages in my home included that men were never to show weakness, must be physically tough and emotionally detached to survive, and that the man in the family had the advantage, both economically and physically. While my family lived in the inner city Projects in New York in my early years, I didn't feel the relative disadvantage of my family's economic status in society at that time. It was what I knew. However within my home, economic and physical advantages held by the man were sources of power that could be used to oppress and even abuse others. Money was used as a tool to control and dominate, and I learned that the female response to this was to feel powerless and shamed. Being female meant to be subjugated; a position in which one could become trapped and without control over one's destiny, a position that should be avoided if at all possible.

I quickly learned that to be male, or at least to internalize stereotypical male traits, meant to minimize vulnerability and avoid the dangers of powerlessness and any associated shame. As a middle sister, I accommodated those messages in ways meant for my brothers and specifically recall the decision to distance myself from the more vulnerable female traits and practice autonomy. Later, as I became part of the working world, I was vigilant against economic disadvantage and continued in my assumed position of autonomy through excessive self-reliance and a focus on professional drive and competitiveness. I had strong reactions, even visceral reactions, to the idea of being "poor." I also had awareness that as a young heterosexual woman with a feminine appearance and style, which I also cultivated and valued, the fierceness of my independence was occasionally confusing to others, in particular interested young men.

In the context of familial messages and the support for those messages within the patriarchal society from which they were derived, I understand my responses to them as adaptive. The tools that I used to manage messages about what it meant to be a woman were developed as a survival strategy and they worked. Later, when I realized those strategies were no longer adaptive in other circumstances, and when I began to crave holism, the skills I had developed in my efforts to be independent, competent, and successful, were the source of the confidence that was necessary for me to begin to reclaim and integrate those feminine qualities previously disavowed.

My empowerment however, was primarily spiritual in nature. Feminist therapists recognize the spiritual realm as a source of empowerment (Brown, 2010). Having strong beliefs in a transcendent God as a child, I explored the Christian scriptures for meaning, identity, guidance, authority (mine), and relationship building with God and others. I practiced yoga and experimented with various forms of meditation, as I sought to grow in peace in 'being' rather than in 'doing.' Growing in spiritual optimism, I explored familial and other factors that influenced my choices, both in and out of therapy, moving towards intrapersonal holism that then contributed to richer interpersonal relationships and deeper life satisfaction.

However, the images I developed of professionals in the working world continued to remain unchallenged for a period of time. In fact, stereotypical masculine traits were valued in the male-dominated world of technology sales and service to which I belonged. Aggressive drive, competitiveness, confidence, and a goal-attainment orientation were well received. They worked and they were rewarded. Eventually however, as my spiritual and psychological optimism and satisfaction grew, my professional life began to feel stale. Empowered by the changes I had made, and passionate about my desire to participate in some way in the healing and empowerment process of others, I entered the world of psychology. It was then that my professional role-schema was challenged.

THE MENTORING RELATIONSHIP

I did as Kathryn suggested and went to see her at her office at the school for which she was President and Dean, the American University of Complementary Medicine. Upon entering, I was greeted by a great statue of Buddha, soothing waterfall sounds, and colorful Hindu art. In addition to her Ph.D. in Clinical Psychology, Kathryn had obtained a Doctorate of Homeopathic Medicine. As I came to know her better, it was clear that her commitment to clinical work, whether through use of psychology, Ayurveda, homeopathy, or traditional Chinese medicine, was an extension of her generous spirit and her belief that holistic treatment was the most appropriate approach to treating all human distress, even when it required that one stray from the predominately dualistic approach traditionally taught in Western academic institutions. I would also come to see that infused throughout her practice was love and a heart of service for both humanity and the divine. Under her supervision, I began a part time psychologist assistantship and taught a psychology course to the school's alternative medicine practitioners.

As soon as the dust settled in my new position(s), she announced: "I want you to take this training" and soon thereafter, "No, I cannot reimburse you. Can you do it?" The training that Kathryn referred to was in a particular intervention used to resolve neurological imbalances resulting from stress and trauma. Intrigued by the idea of a mind-body treatment with which she had so much success, and maybe even more interested because of its specifically unorthodox nature, I was excited to learn more. Of course I could do it.

However, a product of a scholar/practitioner model in my graduate training, I questioned its use in clinical practice. Was it empirically validated? Was it considered experimental? Could it harm anyone? Could I be sued? We discussed the literature on the effectiveness of psychotherapy in general, the importance of my own comfort in providing this or any treatment to my patients, her supervision of the techniques, the potential use of an additional informed consent, and ultimately, the wellbeing and benefit of the patient. As appropriately, she challenged me, "if you come to believe that you have something to offer that will help relieve someone's distress, can you in good conscience withhold it from your patient because you have yet to see the data?" No, I could not. Despite that my passion for my work arose from spiritual as well as psychological growth, and an ever-evolving movement towards holistic integration within my personal identity, I had yet to draw fully and authentically on my experiences and lessons learned as part of my professional identity. In addition to familiarizing myself with empirically validated therapies, this realization led me to begin the practice of accessing my heart, my spirit, my connection to God, and listening to and trusting my own intuition in the context of my clinical work.

At the training, when listening to the presenter teach the triune brain theory, I noted some inaccuracies in the didactic portion of the seminar. The presenter at that time was very well known and in fact was of some celebrity status in certain circles and the inaccuracies were minor without impact to the treatment itself, so I dismissed them. As they continued however, I turned to Kathryn who had accompanied me to the training and whispered "that's not right- what he's saying. That's not true and not what the theory indicates." She said simply "Yes. Challenge him." Indeed. There was more to her than I knew. Her assertion that he be challenged was without ego or competitiveness. As empowered as I was in my previous work, I realized that I did not yet enjoy that same confidence in my new career, at least not to the degree that I would have spontaneously and independently challenged a well-known male authority figure in the process of lecturing a room packed full of other clinicians. And so I did.

As a new teacher to alternative medicine practitioners and a clinician with a small caseload in her practice, under Kathryn's supervision I learned about the philosophies underlying the practice of Eastern healing techniques, and how "dis-ease" was often explained by a number of variables that we do not typically assess or treat in psychology or medical practice in the United States. While a proponent of empirically validated therapies, Kathryn encouraged a broader approach to case conceptualization than those found in the textbooks and manuals, and challenged me to consider the patient's contextual nuances in selecting any approach to my clinical interactions. As a new therapist with a somewhat overly committed orientation to the science of psychology, this was valuable to consider. Another lesson learned was in how I dealt with countertransference. Knowing that I was a practicing Christian, when presented with difficult clinical patients that engendered countertransference, she suggested I consider my beliefs about God's love for every soul and whether I believed they were all created equal. An intervention that had personal and spiritual meaning to me, this became a very valuable strategy to managing countertransference. She challenged me to dig deep for empathy in those cases and find "that thing" to connect to, whatever form that may take.

Eventually the progression of my training required that I accepted a full time internship elsewhere. I continued to see a small caseload of patients in Kathryn's private practice one evening per week. This transition was associated with a change in our relationship. Kathryn began to assume more of a role as mentor than supervisor. Galbraith and Zelenack (1991) define mentoring as "a powerful emotional and passionate interaction whereby the mentor and protégé experience personal, professional, and intellectual growth and development." Golian and Galbraith (1996) note that "informal mentoring is a relationship that occurs that is unplanned, and, in most cases, not expected. A certain "chemistry" emerges drawing two individuals together for the purpose of professional, personal, and psychological growth and development. Informal mentoring seems to be a qualitative experience that has great meaning for the parties involved, (p. 102). As the relationship continued to evolve into one characterized by mutuality and Kathryn's increasing but judicious transparency, I believe it to be a relationship that was valuable to us both.

Initially, Kathryn provided me with encouragement and guidance in my professional growth, and soon thereafter, my spiritual growth. As the protégé, our time together was usually focused on my career choices, and professional options. Kathryn provided particularly valuable guidance in the navigation of difficult systems and personalities within organizational hierarchies. Over time, we came to know one another better. As mature, white women with Christian beliefs and values we had much in common. As our relationship deepened, we also grew in awareness of our differences.

For instance, on the surface, our personalities were quite different. She was thoughtful, soft spoken and gentle, while I am outgoing, and often effusive enough to be verbally impulsive when excited. In truth, sometimes I felt somewhat frustrated by her tranquility, given my own exuberance. Yet I knew she had passion underneath that rivaled my own and that I respected. She in turn accepted my own extroversion with grace, patience, and sometimes amusement.

In time, the mutuality of our relationship became more evident and the bond between us strengthened. She noted some of her own difficult career choices, and shared her efforts to balance competing demands. We shared a love of French pastry and Northern Italian food and made attempts in our limited window of time together to connect over lunch or dinner. There we talked about our love for animals, including each of us in turn sharing our sorrows as first hers, and then my beloved pet passed away. We talked about relationships, career demands and choices, clinical work, and most often, matters of a spiritual nature. Whatever the topic of conversation, the connection itself was what I came to look forward to when I made my way to West Los Angeles to meet with Kathryn.

AMMAS AND THE MOTHER-HEALER ARCHETYPE

I was a non-denominational Christian when I returned to school to become a psychologist. At the time, I had Evangelical leanings in that I wanted others to share in the joy that I experienced in my conversion (from early childhood Catholicism). I believed that the most appropriate, respectful, and effective way for this to occur was for the changes affected by my beliefs and my relationship with God, merely to be visible to others, and that the 'witness' of my story should be further offered if it was asked of me. I still believe this to be true. However my story, informed by new insights and the ongoing evolution of my thinking about what Christianity means, has changed.

My understanding of the divine as a Christian was a personal one. Despite that the scriptural language, and cultural and political world in the days of Christ reflected an overtly patriarchal context, the image I had of Jesus included his love for and respect of women as informed by stories learned in my childhood, indeed stories that I accessed regularly as they transcended the exaggerated traditional masculine messages to which I was exposed at the time. The images included Jesus's love for Mary Magdalene, his compassion for the adulteress, his humility in washing the feet of his disciples, and his empathy in meeting people where they were in an effort to teach and inspire. So, the image of Jesus "in the flesh" had great power for me. Given previous spiritual experiences that I had as I worked on my own healing (Ruff, 2011), I had become interested in and actively explored Christian mysticism and transpersonal conceptualizations of the divine, while continuing to access a personal relationship with God. My spiritual curiosity and Kathryn's own spiritual journey were the subject of many of our conversations.

Kathryn likened her spiritual beliefs to those that she called the "original Christians." In the early days of Christianity, the Desert Mothers (*ammas*—translated 'mothers' but also indicating wisdom, guidance, and care of souls; Earle, 2007, p. 4) of Northern Egypt devoted themselves to cultivating *Christ Consciousness* by communing with God while living in relative isolation from others and devoting themselves to prayer. However, they were often called on to minister, and offer hospitality, to traveling guests who came to their doorsteps. Indeed they believed that they were not living up to their full human potential if not extending the love of God in service to those who were hungry, lonely, sick or otherwise suffering in some way. They eventually became known for their counsel to others, coming to be called "lovers of souls" (Earle, 2007).

The ammas were also subversive. In the 4th century, the average life expectancy during the Roman Empire was 25 years, with few living beyond 50. The pressure on young women to marry and bear children was tremendous. Yet the ammas took radical steps to leave the comforts of their neighborhoods and cities and the cultural pressure to procreate, to create lives in the wilderness where they were better able to hear God. Sometimes they lived in communities with other women, and sometimes they sought solitude (Earle, 2007). Chryssavgis (2003) describes this landscape; "the desert is a place of spiritual revolution, not of personal retreat. It is a place of inner protest, not outward peace. It is a place of deep encounter, not of superficial escape. It is a place of repentance, not recuperation." Still they exemplified their love of God in their service to others and balanced silence, prayer, and relative solitude with guidance, healing, hospitality, charity, and their well-known refusal to judge others.

Perhaps the depths of their inner strengths should not be too surprising when one considers their heritage. The ammas arose from their foremothers who lived prior to the legalization of Christianity by the Emperor Constantine (Earle, 2007). They were not considered equal to men, (although they were generously given dominion over the home), yet rather than denounce their faith, they submitted to torture and execution as courageously as the heartiest of their male martyr counterparts. Despite their tremendous courage, remarkable spiritual commitment, and exceptional modeling of putting divine love into daily practice, the stories of these powerful women whose practice persisted into Medieval Western Europe, were often dismissed entirely due to the hostility towards women in the early Church Fathers (Margot, 2003), or simply by being overshadowed by them (Earle, 2007).

Kathryn meditated in prayer daily in an expression of her willingness to commune with the divine, and in symbolic openness to the action of God in her life, while always striving to move in the direction of Christ Consciousness. Like the desert Mothers, she lived out her faith and love in her everyday personal and professional life. Since I had not yet fully integrated the valuable female elements of my personal identity into my developing professional identity when we first began work together, Kathryn's modeling of this integration was powerful. The connection between us deepened as it became evident to us both that the nature of her values was similar to those that I also embraced and considered spiritually essential.

Aware of my interest in Christian mysticism, Kathryn guided my exploration of the literature to classics such as St. John of the Cross's *Dark Night of the Soul* (1619/2003), *The Cloud of Unknowing & The Book on Privy Counseling* (unknown author, 1375/1973), and what would become a favorite, St. Teresa of Avila's *The Interior Castle* (1577/2003). In *The Interior Castle*, St. Teresa interprets a vision that she believed represented the seven stages of faith which ultimately culminated in union with God. While captivated by her poetic description of these phases as I traversed my own, I too had an experience that I believed was divinely inspired. One of several that I had over the years, this would be the first time I chose to share it with someone else. I, like many others who have had similar experiences, often decide not to disclose them to others because of the inherent difficulty in conveying the essence of such an experience with language when the experience or the insight gained was not received or understood in language. There was also the matter of not being believed in one's conviction that the experience was divine in nature, or divinely inspired. Nevertheless, as I inadequately but with much enthusiasm attempted to recount this experience to Kathryn, she responded by exclaiming with quiet delight and a hint of surprise "St Teresa has given you a gift." She understood the meaning of the experience to me, accepted it as such without question, and as such could not have honored it any more completely.

MOVING ON

Our relationship lasted for only a few years. Time passed and I would move away to be married and live in a small town and work on my dissertation full time. Before leaving, I processed some of my anxiety about such a big step over a plate of steaming risotto on a restaurant patio on a beautifully bright and sunny Los Angeles day. Anxiety notwithstanding, Kathryn declared it an "adventure" and we toasted to my success. Vowing to stay in touch, we parted ways.

We stayed in touch from a distance for a year or two after my relocation, but that too faded as we went about the business of living daily life. Soon thereafter, tasked with navigating other changes such as graduation, licensure, and yet another relocation for work, I realized I had slowly moved away from the spiritually focused part of my life that had been so important to me. I happened upon a Christian Contemplative Prayer retreat in the local mountains of Central California. I attended the retreat and learned about and practiced the meditative method of deepening my relationship with God and inviting him into my everyday life. In my study and practice, I realized that this was the meditation of which Kathryn spoke, and an approach to communing with God similar to that of the ammas. Practicing Contemplative Prayer was key in helping me re-engage my spiritual identity.

My spiritual re-engagement prompted memories of our conversations and the enjoyment that I felt connecting with her in our mutual passion for matters of the spirit, clinical work, or any number of topics. When the opportunity arose to write about Sisters of the Heart, I thought about her profoundly generous and loving spirit that impacted me on so many levels. I recalled how she shared her experiences, and modeled the values she claimed. I remembered her encouragement and guidance in exploring those things I was most passionate about; meaning, purpose, choosing my spiritual path and living with intention, and also indulging in laughing, crying, and dining with passion. Excited about the prospect of honoring the relationship by writing about it, I decided to call her and discuss it with her over dinner. Sadly, I was never able to have that conversation with Kathryn. In my efforts to reconnect, I learned that she had passed away.

IN THE LONG TERM

My relationship with Kathryn began as I was developing as a new psychologist. As is often the case with others, my mentor experience was influential in furthering the development and integration of my personal and professional identity (Green & Hawley, 2009), rather than specific clinical strategies (Tamasine, 1998). As a mentor, Kathryn modeled a harmonious balance of empathy, patience, compassion, and relationships with independence, and professional and personal competence and success. I respected and even emulated that balance as a psychologist new to the field. In particular, that modeling influenced the integration of personal dimensions of my identity, some of which were previously relegated to the shadows and only recently reclaimed, into my professional identity.

My experience of having a woman mentor was similar to those reported by others (Nevels & Coche, 1993) who noted more intimacy and connectedness with their women mentors compared to their men mentor counterparts. In her discussion of women mentors for females, authors recognize the special bond between women and their female mentors. They cite one woman; "with males [mentors] what was valuable was learning to be more demanding of self and others. With females [mentors], generally bonding, learning by example, allowing myself to really study them-and their allowing me to do so" represented a more collaborative interaction. Within this intimate relationship, hierarchies are generally contraindicated. Trust is gained through relationships that value characteristics such as mutuality, empathy, acceptance, and respect. Self-congruence is evident and transparent modeling a valuable method of empowerment.

Kathryn's transparency and modeling of authentic values such as respect, compassion, acceptance, love, and a spiritually rooted commitment to service, encouraged my freedom to carefully and without judgment examine my own values, strengths, challenges, and preferences in developing my own professional style and clinical approach with my patients. Many of these characteristics are in fact key to transformative psychotherapy. I came to internalize them as accessible and necessary characteristics for effective clinical work and believe they engender a sense of safety, increased mutuality and respect, and provide a platform for healing to occur in my patients.

Jean Baker Miller (1986) discusses the developmental importance of relationships in general in *The Five Good Things*. She postulates that empowerment, clarity, vitality, a sense of self-worth, and increased desire for other relationships, arise from relationships that facilitate growth. Moreover, as women, we intuitively seem to know the value of relationships and often seek out other women with whom to connect. Recent research supports what many of us already knew; that relationships with other women are beneficial. One study (Tannen, 2010) noted that it is the connection itself, rather than the content of conversations between women that is beneficial. Other research (Padilla-Walker, Harper, & Jensen, 2010) indicates that even having a sister while growing up is negatively related to internalizing behaviors (turning emotions inward), a result that researchers also credit as a benefit of the relationship.

The benefits of women's mentor relationships include increased self-esteem and productivity, and career advancement, while challenges include access to women mentors in male dominated fields, and collusion in stereotypical roles. These and other variables are discussed in the literature (Bogat & Redner, 1985; Dreher, Cox, & Taylor, 1996; Gilbert & Rossman, 1992; Green & Hawley, 2009; Hansman, 1998; Nevel & Coche, 1993; Paludi, Martin, Stern, and Defour, 2011; Ragis & Cotton, 1999; Ulku-Steiner, Kurtz-Costes, & Kinlaw, 2000) with recent work that discusses mentoring of African American women underrepresented in research and academia (Daniel, 2009; Evans & Cokley, 2008) and mentoring of Latinas (Comas-Diaz, 2011; Gonzalez-Figueroa & Young, Angela, 2005) and Asian-American women (Homma-True, 2011) in various professional roles. While there is some growing literature on strategies and models for mentoring women (Chesler & Chesler, 2002; Files, Blair, Mayer, & Ko, 2008; Liang, Tracey, Taylor, & Williams, 2002; Rayburn, Denmark, Reuder, & Austria, 2011; Williams-Nickelson, 2009), an increase in attention to the topic is indicated.

Women are encouraged to participate in mentor-mentee relationships, which can often be initiated and developed in professional environments or organizations. Experienced women clinicians have the ability to offer a legacy of wisdom to other women through the mentor-mentee relationship. As a mutual participant, mentors are also likely to be rewarded by the relationship, and derive a sense of satisfaction from the generative process.

Finally, according to Mary Reuder (2010), a mentoring relationship is akin to a close friendship since a mentor is "a friend in deed" (p. 194).

CONCLUSION

While writing this narrative in homage to my mentor and friend and feeling her absence in my heart, I easily recall the passion I had in those days for new lessons and insights, and how I looked forward to learning and connecting in our time together. In so doing, I realized it has been several years since I'd read St Teresa of Avila's *The Interior Castle* (1577/2003). Remembering the enthusiasm with which I devoured St. Teresa's analysis, the spiritual experience that I had while reading it, and Kathryn's empathic recognition of it as a gift that I had been given; I retrieved it from my bookshelf. Holding the familiar and beloved text, it fell open to reveal a Christmas card-turned-bookmark tucked away within the pages. I opened the card and read the note inside: "Jennifer, may the Consciousness of Christ and the great saints be born in you this Christmas and every day. Love Kathryn." The gift of my mentor relationship, and ultimately my friendship and spiritual sisterhood with Kathryn, also continues to live on in my heart and spirit, as it does in my life's work.

REFERENCES

Armaroli, C., Constantini, F. G., Malacarne, C., & Mich, O. (2004). Gender in information technology: Review of a mentoring initiative. In C. A. Brebbia & A. Voiskounsky (Eds.), *Human perspectives in the internet society: culture, psychology and gender* (pp. 209–216). WIT Press. Retrieved from http://library.witpress.com/pages/advsearchres.asp

Bogat, G. A., & Redner, R. L. (1985). How mentoring affects the professional development of women in psychology. *Professional Psychology: Research and Practice, 16*(6), 851–859.

Chesler, N. C., & M. A. (2002). Gender-informed mentoring strategies for women engineering scholars: On establishing a caring community. *Journal of Engineering Education, January*, 49–55.

Chryssavgis, J. (2003). *The heart of the desert: The spirituality of the Desert Fathers and Mothers.* World Wisdom Books: Bloomington, IN.

Comas-Diaz, L. (2011). Madrinas, comadres, and luminarias: Latina mentors in action. In C. A. Rayburn, F. L. Denmark, M. E. Reuder, & A. M. Austria (Eds.), *A handbook for women mentors* (pp. 161–171). Santa Barbara, CA: Praeger.

Cushman, A. (1991). Are all women healers? *Yoga Journal.* January/February 1991

Daniel, J. H. (2009). Next generation: A mentoring program for Black female psychologists. *Professional Psychology: Research and Practice, 40*(3), 299–305.

Dreher, G. F., Cox, Jr., & Taylor, H. (1996). Race, gender, and opportunity: A study of compensation attainment and the establishment of mentoring relationships. *Journal of Applied Psychology, 81*(3), 297–308.

Earle, M. C. (2007). *The Desert Mothers: Spiritual practices from the women of the wilderness*. Morehouse Publishing: Harrisburg, NY.

Ehrenreich, B., & English, D. (1973). *Witches, midwives, and nurses: A history of women healers*. New York: The Feminist Press at the City of University of New York.

Evans, G. L., & Cokley, K. O. (2008). African American women and the academy: Using career mentoring to increase research productivity. *Training and Education in Professional Psychology, 2*(1), 50–57.

Files, J. A., Blair, J. E., Mayer, A. P., & Ko., M. G. (2007). Facilitated peer mentorship: A pilot program for academic advancement of female medical faculty. *Journal of Women's Health, 17*(6), 1009–1015.

Galbraith, M. W., & Zelenak, B. S. (1991). Adult learning methods and techniques. In M. W Galbraith (Ed.), *Facilitating adult learning: A transactional process* (pp. 103–133). Malabar, FL: Krieger Publishing.

Gilbert, L. A., & Rossman, K. M. (1992). Gender and the mentoring process for women: Implications for professional development. *Professional Psychology: Research and Practice, 23*(3), 233–238.

Golian, L. M., & Galbraith, M. W. (1996). Effective mentoring programs for professional library development. In D. Williams & E. Garten (Eds.), *Advances in library administration and organization* (PP. 95–124). Greenwich, CT: JAI Press.

Gonzalez-Figueroa, E., & Young, A. M. (2005). Ethnic identity and mentoring among Latinas in professional roles. *Cultural Diversity and Ethnic Minority Psychology, 11*(3), 213–226.

Green, A., & Hawley, G. C. (2009). Early career psychologists: Understanding, engaging, and mentoring tomorrow's leaders. *Professional Psychology: Research and Practice, 40*(2), 206–212.

Hansman, C. A. (1998). Mentoring and women's career development. *New Directions for Adult and Continuing Education, 80*(Winter), 63–71.

Homma-True, R. (2011). Mentoring Asian American Women. In C. A. Rayburn, F. L. Denmark, M. E. Reuder, & A. M. Austria (Eds.), *A handbook for women mentors* (pp. 149–59). Santa Barbara, CA: Praeger.

Levant, R. (2011). Research in the psychology of men and masculinity using the gender role strain paradigm as a framework. *American Psychologist, 66*(8), 765–776.

Liang, B., Allison, J. T., Taylor, C. A., & Williams, L. M. (2002). Mentoring college-age women: A relational approach. *American Journal of Community Psychology, 30*(2), 271–288.

Margot, H. K. (2003). The Desert Mothers: A survey of the feminine anchoretic tradition in Western Europe. Peregrina Publishing Co. retrieved from http://hermitary.com/articles/mothers.html

Miller, J. B., & Hartling, L. M. (2011). The development of relational cultural theory. Jean Baker Miller Training Institute. Wellesley Centers for Women. Retrieved from http://www.jbmti.org/Our-Work/the-development-of-relational-cultural-theory

Nevels, L. A., & Coche, J. (1993). *Powerful wisdom: Voices of distinguished women psychotherapists*. San Francisco, CA: Jossey-Bass.

Padilla-Walker, L. M., Harper, J. M., & Jensen, A. C. (2010). Self-regulation as a mediator between sibling relationship quality and early adolescents' positive and negative outcomes. *Journal of Family Psychology, 24*(4), 419–428.

Paludi, M., Martin, J., Stern, T., & DeFour, D. C. (2011). Promises and pitfalls of mentoring women in business and academia. In C. A. Rayburn, F. L. Denmark, M. E. Reuder, & A. M. Austria (Eds.), A handbook for women mentors (79–108). Santa Barbara, CA: Praeger.

Ragis, B., & Cotton, J. L. (1999). Mentor functions and outcomes: A comparison of men and women in formal and informal mentoring relationships. *Journal of Applied Psychology, 84*(4), 529–550.

Reuder, M. E. (2010). A mentor – A friend in deed. In C. A. Rayburn, F. L. Denmark, M. E. Reuder, & A. M. Austria (Eds.), *A handbook of women mentors: Transcending barriers of stereotype, race, and ethnicity* (pp. 189–195). Santa Barbara, CA: Praeger.

Ruff, J. (2011). Adversity, healing, and the development and practice of a woman psychologist. In L. Comas-Diaz & M. Bakur-Weiner (Eds.), *Women psychotherapists; Journeys in healing* (pp. 143–156). Lanham, MD: Jason Aronson.

St. John of the Cross. (2003). *Dark night of the soul.* In E. A. Peers (Translation). Mineola, New York: Dover Publications.

St. Teresa of Avila. (2003). *The interior castle.* In M. Starr (Translation). New York Penguin Group. (Original work published 1577.)

Tamasine, C. G. (1998). *Supervisor mentoring and psychotherapist professional development: An exploratory qualitative study* (Doctoral dissertation). Available from ProQuest Dissertation and Theses database. (AAI9830593).

Tannen, D. (2010). Why sisterly chats make people happier. The New York Times, October 25, retrieved from http://www.nytimes.com/2010/10/26/health/26essay.html

Ulku-Steiner, B., Kurtz-Costes, B., & Kinlaw, C. R. (2000). Doctoral student experiences in gender-balanced and male dominated graduate programs. *Journal of Educational Psychology, 92*(2), 296–307.

Unknown author. (1973). *The cloud of unknowing & the book of privy counseling.* In W. Johnston (Ed.), New York: DoubleDay. (Original work published 1375.)

Williams-Nickelson, C. (2009). Mentoring women graduate students: A model for professional psychologists. *Professional Psychology: Research and Practice, 40*(3), 299–305.

Sister of the Heart and Mind: Healing and Teaching with Family System Constellations

JANICE CRAWFORD

Private Practice, New York, New York

This article honors the author's mentor, Suzi Tucker, a major contributor to Hellinger's systemic family constellation work. The current understanding of empathy is expanded to include multi-generational systemic empathy. Further, in this paradigm the relationship to the mother represents the relationship to the body and to life itself, and an intimate glimpse is offered of how Tucker also assisted the author toward completing the critical reaching-out gesture toward her own mother and ultimately to both lineages. In this way, the teacher – student relationship becomes a sister of the heart connection. As obstacles to receiving the most enduring source of strength and love are resolved, an even more trustworthy maturity develops that represents new possibilities for feminist therapeutic success.

INTRODUCTION

Knowing Suzi Tucker and her work can be mystifying and even somewhat destabilizing. However, as it was for me, it can also be a gateway to an indescribable relief and a level of perception not yet imagined.

Annette's Panic Disorder

An immediately likeable 50-year-old psychoanalyst, Annette entered my office several months ago in a state of barely controlled panic. Describing what sounded like a well-traveled diagnosis, she said she had been "too enmeshed with her mother." She also said she was in the process of leaving her analysis of 17 years and was interested in exploring Peter Levine's Somatic Experiencing (SE) trauma work (Levine, 2010). She was unaware that like a growing number of clinicians around the world (St. Just, 2008; Schmidt, 2006) my work represents a marriage of Levine's approach with that of Bert Hellinger and, in my case, my training in the last six years with Suzi Tucker, a master facilitator of Hellinger's systemic family constellation work.

In order to not further activate the more primitive part of Annette's nervous system by recounting and thus reliving her most intense fears, I asked her little about her panic attacks or traumatic experiences. We spent a good deal of time establishing her impressive emotional and spiritual resources. However, a few questions made it quickly clear that, with the exception of one sister, she adamantly indicated those resources did not include her family of origin. Fortunately Annette had developed an excellent capacity to track sensations in her body, and we did some initial SE "pendulation" or moving her awareness from and verbally describing quieter or more parasympathetic neutral places in the body to the edge of activation of the sympathetic freeze. As she was able to do this a gentle trembling release began, and leaving she said, "I feel encouraged that I can find islands of calm in my body and experience the ground beneath me more than I expected."

In the second session, she said that she found a place inside to observe what was occurring within and was finding herself more interested "in the sensing part of my life." She also reported now that a sibling, Tommy, three years older than she, died when she was six years old and that the family had fragmented after his death. Her father, she said, "dissolved." Leaving the family soon after Tommy's death, it would be many years before she and her father reconciled. She described her mother as very anxious and "always moving." As grief possessed her after her son's death, her mother's love "never returned." Describing these events it was clear she was reliving this trauma and speaking as the six-year-old child frozen in time. Tommy, she said, was seldom mentioned after his death, a "conspiracy of silence" that traumatologist Yael Danieli proposes "is the most prevalent and effective mechanism for the transmission of trauma on all dimensions" (Danieli, p. 678). And as we concluded this session Annette said she knew she needed to leave her long-term partner but was terrified: "I won't be able to survive." She reported that even the work with her beloved analyst had not resolved her core terror of death and separation.

In my earlier years as a Self Psychological Psychoanalyst, I would have explored Annette's feelings of loss, abandonment and disrupted attachment, probably for a considerable time, perhaps years. Further, I would have more fully accepted my client's narrative as the basic truth, perhaps not noticing there was a deeper level of reality here or the level on which she had obvious doubts about that story herself. At that time I believed that my role was to step into a transferential parental position to help her complete developmental movements with me. And in more recent years I would have approached Annette's panic attacks from a more somatic than intersubjective level, focusing on helping her body find a greater capacity for mature self-regulation and pleasure.

Guided as well now, however, by Suzi's encouragement to "Extend the latitude of what fullness is" (personal communication), I also knew that the intensity of Annette's rejection of both parents and the distortion of Tommy's right place in the family soul, particularly when she was activated into these regressions, represented the most fundamental traumatic obstacle to her sustainable strength and stability. Therefore, if Annette chose to continue, a major part of our work would be to discover her own particular path to the level on which she could connect to her present family and historical family. I knew now that she could as Suzi says, "reclaim love" and resolve those obstacles directly with the excluded person or a representative of that person—even when they are deceased—and that I was the least important link in that chain.

Beginning her next session Annette said, "I am beginning to feel the pilot light in my core." And having introduced a bit of orientation to Hellinger's insights in each of Annette's sessions, I then asked her if she was willing to take her time and put a pair of felt footprints on the floor to represent her mother and a pair to represent herself. She walked slowly around the center of the middle of the room and placed the footprints about five feet apart, facing in opposite directions away from the center of the field.

After Annette quietly observed the feeling of this image for a time, she moved her footprints beside her mother to her mother's right and stood in them, facing in the same direction as her mother. Diagnostically the position Annette placed herself in was the enmeshment position she had been stuck in for most of her life and was the position constellations have shown to be the place of the father. I then asked her to just notice any general sensations. I asked whether she felt stable or shaky, what direction her eyes might be drawn or whether she felt drawn in a particular direction. And as she sensed into her body she immediately felt there was "something wrong" and said, "I want Tommy between us!"

When I placed footprints for Tommy between Annette and her mother, also facing in the same direction, Annette's body immediately began to significantly relax. Leaning to the left into the virtual Tommy, she began to weep and said, "He loved me. He really loved me." It appeared that because the grief over Tommy's death had been too much for the family to bear, Annette had been waiting decades to be able to acknowledge this. And after a time of honoring what was unfolding I said to her "Even with Tommy standing between you and the three of you facing in the same direction, you (and your mom) may not feel complete relief."

Recognizing now that being close to Tommy felt wonderful but that this position in relation to her mother still did not feel right, she explored my guidance and stood about four feet across from and facing her mother. I placed Tommy's footprints beside Annette with both now facing their mother. In this position reaching toward the parent and receiving from her is not enmeshment. Rather, here Annette is in the right place—her place as a child—and actually completing necessary movements that lead to turning toward the future with her parents and lineages behind her. Her body and some might say soul clearly rested into some deeper comfort here, and after a few minutes I asked if it would be alright with her to bring her father's footprints in and place them to the right of her mother (in whose place she had originally been standing) with both her parents facing her and Tommy. We then gently looked at this together in silence for quite some time, and it appeared life was finally falling into place, reflecting its deeper reality for the first time in many decades.

Suzi describes these moments of resolution in "The Weight of Words" (Tucker, 2005):

> "Out of the stuff of collective life, all of our family systems (and beyond them too), there emerges the interstitial reality that cannot be manipulated by narrative. It comes and it shows itself and we know. Words are ancillary, sometimes even detrimental, to this level of movement." (p. 9)

Because these constellations affect one on a level other than the cognitive and should not be subjected to immediate analysis, Annette and I did not discuss what had just occurred. However, when she left the session it was clear some sea change had begun. And in the next session she began by saying she and her partner of ten years had decided to separate. She also said she had allowed herself to receive support from her parents. As she experienced them solidly behind her she said, "They are showing an understanding for the pain I am going through and a confidence in my strength I could never have imagined." Expressing enormous gratitude to her analyst she said she was also beginning to conclude her analysis. She also said she was enjoying committing more seriously to her spiritual work.

In our most recent session Annette said that though it was sometimes painful, she and her partner had also been able to lovingly grieve together about the ending of their relationship. She was soft and open, and there was a pervasive calm in the room. Saying very little, we sat together with that feeling. Annette then said that for the first time in her meditation practice her body and mind were beginning to find periods of comfort. She stated, "I am beginning to enjoy silence." In a better position with her mother and father, she could afford to be more inclusive and compassionate. And here she could begin to hold all the grief and love that until now she had felt would overwhelm her. She had done a great deal of work before these sessions, and it's very important to say the constellation work with Annette was not magic. With as little intention as I could manage I simply let myself explore what might be offered by forces larger than I, knowing that if we allowed it the work could move toward clarifying and beginning to resolve dynamics that may have been carried in her family for generations.

As Annette well knows, there will continue to be bumps and temporary detours in the road to these new reference points for systemic stability. However, since from a Hellinger perspective the way we relate to our mother's is the way we relate to our bodies and life itself, having become more aligned, particularly with her mother, she will increasingly be an even more trustworthy partner and therapist. She has gotten a glimpse of a reality that I have seen emerge with people from every race and imaginable cultural background. Here we let the locked places in our psyches be slowly transformed to allow the existence of another dimension where there is no interest in blame or judgment. Here the recurring fact is that no matter what their entanglements were or are, those behind us love us.

There can be many clarifying movements ahead if Annette chooses to explore this work further. One place to explore in a constellation might be her father and mother's particular ways of negotiating life. In her father's case, for example, we might pose the question, "What might have left my father unable to grieve and stay within the family?" Another constellation might explore generationally what might cause her mother to be "always moving." Or Annette might attend one of Suzi's groups and explore these or other issues with group members standing in to represent relevant people in her life.

In what Jung called the "collective consciousness" and evolutionary biologist Rupert Sheldrake (2009) has called the "morphogenic field," in constellation circles as people step in to "represent" others we see that we all know a great deal we didn't know we know. As this occurs the facilitator and group acquire greater levels of what one might call multigenerational systemic competence in relation to the client, an overarching perspective that includes what Comas-Diaz (2012) describes as cultural competence. And unlike psychodrama, with little or no information about whom or what they are representing, they are often asked to simply follow their sensations. For example, do they sense a movement toward or away from someone else? Do they feel unstable or strong? And what is still remarkable to me after seeing thousands of constellations with participants from 47 different nations is—anyone can do this.

Because this work obviously requires some expansion of conventional ways of thinking, a few sessions into our work Annette spoke about a concern: "I'm afraid of what the work with you might question about my way of working with clients. However, I did notice that though I am equally empathic to their feelings (emphasis hers) and real experiences of, for example, abandonment or rejection, I am beginning to see and hold for them and with them something more." And for me it is primarily Suzi who helps me see there is always something more.

Having no intention of becoming my new and better mother, Suzi holds a global respect for my mother and my whole family system in ways I only sometimes could. A painter, writer and editor of most of Hellinger's books in English, she facilitates constellations in the United States and Canada. And in a poem I wrote several years into this work, "Until Today" (Crawford, 2010), I said that I had looked "in many faces and many faiths" for what I was finding now in my mother' s eyes—and in a later constellation, in my father's now believable embrace—because of my work with her.

With the exception of my youngest brother, I had politely rejected everyone behind me and got as far away as soon as I could. Even after decades of psychotherapy and psychoanalysis, it wasn't until I saw human beings stand in the places of my family members and respond in ways far outside my narrative that my embedded primal rejections began to shift. The following excerpt is from my book in progress. It was facilitated for me by Suzi and represents a step in the shift with my mother and life:

"With obvious collapsing energy as I relived the experience in my memory I began by saying that I felt in my childhood as if "I was living in a desert in many ways, a god-forsaken place where nothing could grow." Suzi then asked someone in the circle if they would represent "Yes" to life and someone else if they would represent "No." A third person was placed in the circle to represent me.

When Jan stepped in she was immediately frightened, walking nervously around Yes. Suzi then asked a female group member to enter to represent my Mother. Asked to follow her movement, she stood behind Jan. Then Suzi asked another representative whose identity was not revealed to enter the circle. That representative immediately moved toward Yes and took Yes's hand. Saying that until that moment she had felt frozen, Yes said, "I can now begin to feel my own heart." With Mother now behind her Jan then started spontaneously moving slowly toward Yes, and the unidentified representative then stepped behind Jan's Mother in the place of Mother's mother. With that Mother appeared visibly stronger. Invited now to replace the representative for Jan, I moved into my place and began to shed tears of relief.

A few days later Suzi sent me an e-mail with the photo of a golden poppy surrounded by sage, reminding me how exquisite a desert flower can be. By then fortunately a few more molecules of the force of life had begun to flow in my veins, and I could feel the truth and promise of those words.

Having had the pleasure of being in a study group with the brilliant intersubjectivity theorist Jessica Benjamin in the early 1990s, I anticipate some feminists, including Jessica, would be alarmed at what might appear to be my attempt to "restore a lost maternal or feminine order on the margins of culture and to avoid the dark side of maternal power" (Benjamin, 1995,

p. 107). And I can only say briefly here that in this work both parents are seen in the widest dimension of themselves, acknowledging all that is true. Further, it has been my growing experience that until one can perceive what has been excluded about these more benevolent layers of reality, one cannot move into maturity. This, however, sometimes involves strong direction to explore new positions and perspectives.

And though Suzi usually works with exquisitely aligned gentleness, at 5-foot-2 and 17 years my junior, it is also true that she can occasionally carry a powerfully precise delusion-destroying strong direction when she needs to. I remember, for example, one piece of group work Suzi set up at my request several years ago. Internally distancing from my grandmothers from an early age I wanted to look at the unspoken though tenacious judgments I felt toward them and the emptiness I felt inside when I thought about them. My paternal grandmother, Betha, lived a few blocks away until I left my hometown at nineteen, and my maternal grandmother, Mary, died ten years before I was born.

Suzi asked me to choose representatives from our Guided Learning group for both of them and for me. And without having any information about the persons they were representing, they stepped slowly into the circle, sensing their basic bodily reactions as they did. I would not until recently know the full story of my grandfather's murder when my father was two years old or the scandal Betha fled in 1929. Having also lost her mother at five and two of her own children, she always appeared to me to be almost catatonic as she sat rocking day and night, totally absorbed in her Bible. And living in often desperate poverty, Mary had given birth to thirteen children with my grandfather who I would learn only in recent years was severely alcoholic and was eventually sent to San Quentin for pedophilia. Several of their children, including my mother who was eleven, were quite young when Mary died and had to be cared for by siblings barely established in their own lives.

The representatives were asked to follow their movements, and it was immediately clear how much sorrow the person representing me felt as she looked helplessly at her two grandmothers. It was obvious she was locked into carrying a huge sadness for them. And it was also evident that these women did not want me to hold their pain and that I, in fact, was not really seeing them. Mary was actually quite strong and vivacious and Betha was looking at me with an undeniable wisdom and kindness I would never have imagined.

Suzi then turned to me and said, "Jan, you have no right to their pain!" And like the awakening slap of the stick in Zen, in that moment my old one-dimensional inner images of Mary and Betha crumbled and expanded far enough to include their wisdom, joy and love for me and all those who followed them. I felt a source of support I do not remember ever having experienced. And there would be so much more. However, because the focus of this article is Suzi's contributions, I will simply say here that in doing Hellinger-inspired work she presupposes that what we are offering is a resonance with the deepest levels of knowing in the client. No matter what entanglements may be occurring on the surface level, on the deepest level clients always have the support of their ancestral family system. The pathology of each system is a given, but we are always looking for the resources, amplifying that part of the family system versus the pathology.

Suzi, Helliinger and several other facilitators of this work help me see the complexity, darkness and beauty of what is beneath the simplistic, justifying and often critical story I, sometimes with the help of loving and skilled psychotherapists trained as I was trained, had developed about my parents and family lineages. Additionally, as I began to see these "movements of the soul," as Hellinger calls them, and to feel the palpable force that seems to guide resolution of "entanglements," it no longer felt so desirable to use words like "clinically depressed mother" or "borderline father," words which with one swipe of the therapeutic sword can reduce a human to one simple often damning diagnosis.

Even if all a mother does is provide a safe enough environment for the child to be born and then risk her life to give birth, she is to be honored. And even if the father is only able to provide the life force of his sperm and therefore his lineage, he has a place. It may be that, as Suzi suggests, either or both of them may have given up their rights as a parent, but they continue to have an irrevocable place in the heart of their child. Further, if that place is not recognized by the child, there will be a fragility that the child attempts to fill from "in front," meaning that he or she asks too much from people and events that cannot possibly fill the hole that is in the past. And for me, no longer enjoying the short-term pleasure of blame or "innocence," as I find the way through to what and who my parents were and continue to be, I increasingly feel life flowing unimpeded through them to me and back to itself.

However much it was a child-created defense against forces I could not influence or understand, my diminishment of my family's love and strength jeopardized my ability to enjoy and pass on the purest intensity of the life force. And in an unpublished poem Suzi describes the effects of these exclusions with the words, "Ancestors wait for the living to see ... the past may reconcile with the future only through the present ... Each blind eye sears the soul." With each constellation I receive, take part in as a representative or even observe I take another step of trusting and loving life. As I discover that as I find my right place among them, everyone in my lineages can be acknowledged, if necessary grieved at last, and honored in a heartfelt way.

In Hellinger's lexicon,

> As to who belongs in the family system and who is embraced by this completeness, it is the following people: the siblings, living and dead [including miscarried or aborted children], the parents and their

> siblings—both living and dead—the grandparents, sometimes, though seldom, one or other of the great-grandparents. If a great grandmother died in childbirth, then she is automatically included. Also included are all those who have made a place for someone else in the system, for example, an earlier husband or wife of the parents or grandparents. If they are all acknowledged and have an acknowledged place in my heart then I will feel rounded and full. (Hellinger, 2006, p. 115)

Some common exclusions from the family soul include a person who met with a special fate like mental illness or physical disability. Homosexuals and other "unacceptable" family members, people whose exploitation benefited the system (i.e. slaves), and others whom the system doesn't have the ability to mourn, from those lost to wars to criminals who are also often excluded. That last category would come to include my maternal grandfather who committed the blindest of crimes, pedophilia. Though I had never met him, when I discovered this family secret I loathed him for his impact on my mother and my family, and I had no idea what this hatred was costing us both.

In encouraging me to stay in a difficult constellation with him Suzi helped me see something that, thankfully, shattered what I righteously thought I knew. I was right on the edge of reactively "fighting" or "fleeing," and she literally held her hand firmly at my back. Because she, Hellinger and several other facilitators as well as my fellow students in groups here and in Spain, Austria and Germany stayed so steadfastly beside me, layers of narrow understandings about my family are being shed, revealing what is infinitely more real and nourishing. Not only who I see when I see them, but what I see when I look in the mirror has changed in the direction of a greater love. And that greater love translates to many things, including a gentle confidence as I interact with clients and their systems. Yes, respect needs to be present for our collaboration to work, but I need nothing on a personal level from them, not adulation, adoration, or even to be "right." I am at peace in ways that I was not previously, having everything I need with me at all times.

I look back and recognize that not being at peace affected how I interpreted the world. As a feminist psychoanalyst, for example, I was the author of a radical and complex gender theory, "The Severed Self: Gender as Trauma" (Crawford, 1996a) that I believe contributed to the exploration of gender that was occurring in the 1980s. I now see it was, however, also overly reductionist and ultimately unkind about masculinity and femininity. Fortunately, despite the radical quality of this theory, I had worked well with men throughout my career. However, it was not until my work with Suzi that I more viscerally understood what it is like for men to be unable to protect life ("guard the periphery" as Suzi calls it) and thereby contribute to life. And seeing men in constellations feel the absence of their connections, often unable to lean back particularly on their male lineages, also has helped me develop a new level of understanding.

Finally, in turning me toward the one heart I share with my entire lineage as we are, my work with Suzi allows me to now say to them without reservation, "Thank you. It was enough." As I more strongly feel that heart-beat I am more aware that when I am not aligned with it I move awkwardly. When I am attuned to it my movements are simple and effortless. And whether I am aligned or not also influences the generations whose life I touch as descendant, aunt, sister, teacher, friend and therapist who now clearly knows her deepest purpose.

REFERENCES

Benjamin, Jessica. (1995). *Like subjects, love objects.* New Haven: Yale University Press.

Comas-Diaz, Lillian. (2012). *Multicultural care: A clinician's guide to cultural competence.* Washington, D.C.: American Psychological Association.

Crawford, Janice. (1996A). The severed self: Gender as trauma. In: A. Goldberg (Ed.), *Basic ideas reconsidered.* Hillsdale, NJ: The Analytic Press.

Danieli, Yael. (1998). *International handbook of multigenerational legacies of trauma.* New York: Plenum Press.

Hellinger, Bert. (2006). *No waves without the ocean.* Heidelberg, Germany: Carl-Auer Systeme Verlag.

Hellinger, Bert. (2008). *Rising in love.* Berchtesgaden, Germany: Hellinger Publications.

Levine, Peter. (2010). *In an unspoken voice.* Berkeley, CA: North Atlantic Book.

Schmidt, Johannes. (2006). *Inner navigation: Trauma, healing and constellation process: Work as navigational tools for evolution of your true self.* Hamburg, Germany: Aptitude-Academy.

Sheldrake, Rupert. (2009). *Morphic resonance.* Rochester, NY: Park Street Press.

St. Just, Anngwyn. (2008). *A question of balance: A systemic approach for understanding and to resolving trauma.* Available from www.booksurge.com

Tucker, Suzi. (2005). The weight of words. In: In S. Tucker and E. Lynch (Eds.), *Messengers of healing: The family constellations of Bert Hellinger through the eyes of a new generation of practitioners.* Phoenix: Zeig, Tucker & Theisen.

Sister Friends: A Reflection and Analysis of the Therapeutic Role of Sisterhood in African American Women's Lives

THEMA BRYANT-DAVIS

Pepperdine University, Malibu, California

Research with ethnically diverse women has found that friendships can enhance women's health and mental wellbeing (Greif & Sharpe, 2010). Sister friends can be crucial in assisting African American women and women of ethnically diverse backgrounds to face, address, and overcome, major transitions including stress and traumatic stress. Through a reflection and analysis of the relationship with a sister friend, the author explores the strength and challenges of sister friendship as well as therapeutic value. Recommendations are provided for sisterhood as a clinical intervention as well as for women therapist's self care. A case study of an African American woman in need of mutual sister friends is summarized. This exploration is shared through a womanistic psychology.

Wholeness, strength, and resilience are central to womanist theory (Williams, 2005). Research with ethnically diverse women has found that friendship can enhance women's health and mental well-being (Greif & Sharpe, 2010). Same–gender relationships can be significant sources of comfort as they provide assistance with emotional support and problem-solving (Samter, Whaley, Mortenson, & Burleson, 1997). Person (2005), in her qualitative study of African American women, notes that female friends play an integral role in socialization, survival, and growth enhancement. This growth enhancement may include educational and occupational advancement. For example, Shaw and Coleman (2000) found in a qualitative study with college enrolled African American females that friends and family played critical roles in providing the support needed for upward mobility. Similar findings occurred in examining the support network of two African American female professors, who were considered "outsiders" in the academy but were able to enhance their success through their connection (Fries-Britt & Kelly, 2005). An earlier study found that African American college educated women report high satisfaction with their female friendships (Godfrey, 1997). These sister friends can be crucial in assisting African American women, and women of ethnically diverse backgrounds, to face, address, and overcome major life transitions, including stress and traumatic stress (Bryant-Davis, 2005; Lincoln, Chatter, & Taylor, 2004; Day, 2004).

I was raised to seek out, celebrate, and empower women. My mother was one of 8 sisters and during my early years she became the minister to women at our Church. She taught women-focused Bible studies, created an AA program, wrote women's devotional books, and started a back to school shoe give away, women's retreats, and women's conferences that have been central to my life from the 70s until today. Throughout my life I have always had a best friend, play sisters, god sisters, pretend cousins. It was not until I was in college that I remember hearing women proclaim proudly that they couldn't stand to be around women. I never knew the internalized sexism that makes women assume that all women are catty, selfish, trifling, untrustworthy, etc. My experience was the opposite. As a child, adolescent, and young woman, it was my female friends who were generous, honest, reliable "home girls." These were the people in whose presence I felt at home, valued, comfortable, and affirmed.

College was not any different. It was my first day on the campus of Duke University—move-in day to be exact. My parents and older brother brought me to campus and we, along with my newly assigned campus big brother, were carrying my belongings up the three flights of stairs all my belongings up the three flights of stairs. It was on our way up the stairs that I met Edith, who would become my lifelong sister. An African American from suburban New York, she also has one older brother and greeted me with a big smile that said "hey sister" immediately. She asked what floor I was on and told me she was on the second floor and rooming with another young Black woman (whose family I knew through my church back in Baltimore). When I told her the third floor, she leaned in and with a grin said there's another Black girl up there named Tosca. This is after all what sisters do. They help to identify safe places, good people, and glimpses of home. They welcome you in even when they are still finding their way around a new place. Needless to say the second floor became my home away from home, especially after we discovered we were both psychology majors.

For African American women social support is an important component for healing and empowerment. It is often sister friends, mothers, grandmothers, aunties, cousins, neighbors, Church mothers, teachers, and even beauticians who are consistent sources of encouragement, guidance, and light. For social support to be effective it needs to be mutually beneficial, grounded in common values/priorities, based in authenticity, accepting, truth-telling, and growth promoting. The social support literature describes both emotional support and instrumental support. There are sister friends who give comfort and then there are those who give resources. At times you may find sister friends who give both.

Edith became a sister for multiple reasons. The first is simply what can be categorized as a spirit connection. I can list a number of traits about her that I appreciate and I will but those traits don't capture the essence of the person. At the core beyond the books we've read, shows we've watched together, valleys we've seen each other through, there is a higher connection, or perhaps a deeper connection that I can simply say is God. Our spirits connect and feel liberated in each other's presence. The ways our faith walk manifest are not identical on the surface but underneath we are on the same journey. Church is a central part of my life and while Edith doesn't go every week her meditation, prayer, and reading connect us spiritually. Our commitment to both personal devotion and a liberation theology of service and uplift tie us together.

We are also sisters because of our common values. We appreciate the gift of our culture and community. In classes we were often the ones who would speak up on issues of race, gender, and economic oppression. Dare I say, we were not the white women written about who lose their voice in mixed gender classrooms. We had lots of opinions (and facts) and were willing to share them. We enjoy thinking, discovering, reading, and writing with a purpose. This I'm sure is due, in no small part, to our parents who raised us both to be aware of the privileges we had as middle-class but to be simultaneously committed to our community as a whole. We were raised with racial consciousness and to understand our responsibility to give back, serve, empower, and uplift those who are marginalized for multiple reasons.

Along with our value for spirituality, community, and education, we also are psychologically minded. We enjoy processing our decisions, actions, words, and lives. We provide for each other open space, safe space, reality checks, and a place to give birth to new ideas as we modify old ideas.

NEW GROWTH

Edith has helped me to grow in multiple ways. One of the most important ways is in stretching me to maintain connections over the years and over a great geographic divide. Having experienced major moves during adolescence as a result of my father's work in the church, I had become accustomed to releasing relationships, no matter how close, pretty easily. Edith's consistent presence in my life over two decades broke this habit for me and helped me to discover how to hold on to people that I value even when it may feel easier to let go. I am so grateful that her presence in my life has given me that gift and lesson.

Another important lesson that Edith inspires in me is the gift of planning ahead. From our college years, she was the one who reminded me that the deadline for GRE's was about to pass. While I am still not as disciplined as she is, whenever I take the initiative of pre-planning, I discover again and again the ways it removes unnecessary stress from my life. I am continuing to evolve in this area and discovering the gift of making life easier for myself.

Our relationship has been about us nurturing each other's survival during difficult times and growth in various aspects of our lives. One of the things Edith has shared appreciating about me was my presence in her life during the time of her dad's passing, especially being present at his wake. Death and loss are experiences for which presence can often do so much more than words. Sisterhood is about showing up even when you don't know what to say. These are the times your presence is most needed.

ROAD BUMP

I can honestly say after much reflection and consulting with Edith that we had many years without a major disagreement or argument. We agree on many issues and on issues we disagree on we can usually at least see each other's perspectives and modify, if not alter, our perspective. Our first and only major divide was leading up to the 2008 Presidential election. I wanted Barak Obama to win and she wanted Hilary Clinton to win. I think we were equally surprised with the other's decision. I know it was difficult for her to feel that she was not able to discuss her feelings regarding the sexism that arose during the campaign with one of her feminist allies whom she usually had such discussions with. Likewise it was difficult for me not to be able to discuss with her the racism in the dismissal of the character and qualifications of then candidate Obama as well as the interlocking issue of White privilege at work during the campaign season.

When it comes down to it, I believe we got through the discomfort because of our respect for each other. In the end, we discussed it some but then mostly left the conversation alone—not trying to sway the other to our vantage point. I will admit on Election Day, she was not among the first calls I made as I wanted to connect with those who I believed were celebrating like me and to also give her space to connect with those who would be more reflective of her mixed feelings about the day's events. She later shared with me that she was celebrating the election of President Obama and that my assumptions that she would be less enthusiastic were not true. In the end it is really about respecting each other's hearts, minds, and politics enough to know our sisterhood outlasts any bumps in the road.

IMPACT OF FRIENDSHIP ON PSYCHOTHERAPY WITH WOMEN

African American women enter therapy having faced challenges with racism, sexism, and multiple forms of oppression such as classism, heterosexism, able-bodyism, and religious intolerance (Bryant-Davis, 2005). Critiques of Afrocentric therapy and feminist therapy have noted the tendency to value and isolate race or gender to the exclusion of other aspects of one's identity, such as the intersection of identity statuses (Williams, 2005). Womanist therapy brings the experiences, needs, and strengths of African American women from the margins of the discourse to the center. The psychological challenges that have been examined in the literature include stress, trauma, racism, isolation, internalized oppression, and the task of integrating multiple identities (Bryant-Davis & Ocampo, 2006; Williams & Wiggins, 2010). Womanist therapeutic strategies for survival and growth have included culture as a resource, spirituality, resistance/activism, and social support, such as the role of friends and family (Williams & Wiggins, 2010). It is important for therapists working with African American women to be aware of these potential challenges as well as the culturally congruent strategies, such as friendship, that may be utilized to overcome these challenges.

There are three primary ways my friendship with Edith has influenced my psychotherapy with women. The first is that I am reminded of the complexity of identity and the nuanced ways that socialization effects our self-conceptualization. I grew up in inner city Baltimore which is predominantly African American, attended predominantly public schools, and have always been a member of a predominantly African American Church. Before Edith my exposure to African Americans who grew up in predominantly White settings was limited and the persons I had encountered often did not hold their African American culture as a central aspect of their identity. Edith absolutely shifted and shattered those assumptions and biases I held. She grew up attending private schools and living in a predominantly White area and was as revolutionary as any sister I have encountered. Edith, largely I would say from the socialization of her parents, drinks books about our culture, works hard to empower African American people, and celebrates the beauty of our people while acknowledging our issues. Her friendship awakened me to the complexity of identity and socialization and the ways these factors are important to the psychotherapy process. The psychotherapist has to constantly be mindful not to categorize, label, or assume we know a person based on a few intake questions. We are layered beings that have been shaped, molded, and inspired by multiple factors that should all be considered.

Edith's friendship also taught me on a personal level the significance of social support. It is invaluable to have someone that knows you fully and accepts you fully. Our friendship represents a safe place, a truth-telling place, and healing place. We can and do process the layered events of our lives. I would want for my clients to have that type of support that is not limited to a therapeutic relationship. I assess for social support being sensitive to not only who they invest in but also who invests in them. Relationships are often unfortunately not mutual. A true sisterhood, authentic friendship has to be based on reciprocity. Along with assessing for social support, I often find myself exploring with clients the possibility of working on building their social support network as a treatment goal.

Additionally, my friendship with Edith is a reminder of the important feminist therapy principle of activism. Many of my conversations with Edith often centers on activism, social justice, and provoking change in ourselves and in the systems in which we find ourselves. Women face multiple forms of trauma, violence, oppression, and stress. These experiences can drain us emotionally and cause a sense of stagnation, powerlessness, and hopelessness. One of the ways of counteracting these potential effects is through direct action. It is empowering to facilitate the process by which those who have been marginalized and silenced rediscover their power and their voices. This is crucial to a therapeutic process that goes beyond symptom cessation to thriving and growth.

A final way that Edith influences my psychotherapy with women is a greater flexibility and acceptance regarding delayed disclosure. Emotionally, culturally, socially, and physiologically, there are a number of issues that are very difficult to discuss. It was months after I had been sexually assaulted that I shared the assault with Edith. Likewise it was years into our friendship that she shared with me some of the details about her family dynamics that she did not often discuss. These delays in disclosure were not because we lacked a connection or genuine trust. We are both people who share over time. The more time passes the more layers we uncover. This is a natural and healthy progression. Likewise when I have been working with a client for some time and suddenly they share something they have been holding, I am able to appreciate the space and time they needed before they were ready to disclose. I honor both the time it takes and the gift of the disclosure as precious and sacred. This requires a slowing down as training programs and managed care often create a climate whereby not having all the pertinent information in the first few sessions is a failure of some sort. To the extent that it is possible, I really try to give clients the safety, space, and time to share at their own pace.

CASE VIGNETTE

Dr. Ebony Johnson is a 40-year-old African American medical doctor who came to see me after experiencing severe panic attacks that made it impossible for her to continue her professional responsibilities. Dr. Johnson grew up witnessing severe family violence and mental illness. Both of her parents died and the grief combined with the unexpressed anger, and depression resulted in the panic. Dr. Johnson had previously coped with stress through her religious faith and with busyness as a source of distraction. Along with being a doctor, she is a wife, mother, gourmet cook, and provider of the neighborhood hang-out for pre-teens. Much of Dr. Johnson's life was spent giving to others and performing her religious, professional, and family duties. There was not space for her to breathe, reflect, or be still.

I assessed her social support and saw there were major gaps in the area of mutually beneficial female friendships. Along with needing to share more with her husband and children, Dr. Johnson began working on setting aside time and emotional space to develop her female friendships. As she began to develop these relationships and to simultaneously challenge some of the myths she had come to believe about herself and others, the panic began to decrease. To demonstrate that this therapeutic goal can be complex and challenging, it is important to note that initially Dr. Johnson came to session reporting about the new mentoring program that she and her sister friend were going to create for the girls at their church. While this may be an eventual project she wants to invest in, it was also important to point out to Dr. Johnson how the time that was supposed to be for her was turning into a brainstorming session of how she can give more of herself away. She was able to see this pattern and to dedicate time to self-care and sisterhood connection without work being involved.

REFLECTIONS

African American women face the stress of racism and sexism, as well as additional forms of oppression that can block their progress. Shorter-Gooden (2004) concludes that strategies that enhance African American women's lives include social support, spirituality, self-awareness, and resistance. Any therapeutic approach that aims to transform mindsets utilizing feminist principles needs to take into account the role and influence of social support. Research has found the protective role that social support can play in the lives of African American women whether facing mental health challenges such as depression and anger or physical health challenges such as smoking, cancer, or HIV (Andrews, Felton, Wewers, Waller, & Tingen, 2007; Edwards, 2006; Simoni, Huang, Goodry, & Montoya, 2005). Social support can be treated as a therapy goal in traditional individual psycho-therapy but also in innovative strategies such as group therapy and expressive arts therapy (Washington, Moxley, & Garriott, 2009). Therapists may integrate the building of sister friend networks by addressing the following with African American female clients:

- Assess the current sister friend network both in terms of quality and quantity. Be mindful that a woman may know a lot of other women but may not automatically be in mutually emotionally beneficial relationships with them. To ascertain the quality of the relationship, the therapist may ask about the length of the relationship, the level of intimacy/sharing in the relationship, the dynamics of their interactions, and the motivation for continuing the friendship.

- Explore and address barriers to engaging in positive sister friend relationships. These barriers may include negative socialization messages about women in general or African American women in particular. The socializing agents may have been family, friends, or even the media. Other barriers may be past negative relationships with women whether these were friends in childhood or adolescence, or even family members. After establishing positive rapport with the client, any cognitive distortions resulting from these negative encounters can be challenged.
- Provide psycho-education about what a healthy friendship looks like. We can never assume that people know the fundamentals of friendship. This can start with being a healthy individual as people may bring their insecurities and personality challenges into their relationships and this can create a toxic relationship. There can also be a discussion and reflection about realistic and healthy expectations to have of one's self and of others. Finally psycho-education about living with balance is needed, as women face multiple demands related to their varied roles and have to consider how to integrate time and energy for the nurturance of healthy sister friendships.

SUGGESTIONS TO WOMEN THERAPISTS

Women therapists are often givers. They tend to give personally and professionally and have to be cautious not to end up drained and stuck in one-sided relationships. The importance of mutuality and reciprocity cannot be over-stated. Women therapists benefit from sister friends. They are integral to personal and professional growth and development. These are the persons in your life that are a source of refreshing, honesty, comfort, and inspiration. The investment of time and energy into developing sister friends is a core component of self-care. These relationships are sites where it is not about "doing" but simply "being you." Without sister friends, women therapists may be at increased risk for burn out and vicarious trauma. As therapists our well-being is critical and should be attended to by engaging with people who help to relieve stress and to protect time for positive, affirming interactions. Three primary recommendations for women therapists are:

- Develop and nurture your sister friendships.
- Encourage your female clients to build healthy sisterhood networks.

- Incorporate the role of sister friends in your research and writing on women's mental health. Research is needed on the formation of female friendships to inform the creation of effective clinical interventions for building social support networks (Greif & Sharpe, 2010).

It should be a feminist/womanist priority to honor the ways women grow, heal, and thrive in our personal lives, in the therapeutic setting, and in our scholarship.

RECOMMENDATIONS TO WOMEN

Women need to combat internalized sexism, as well as other intersecting internalized forms of oppression. This internalization can cause us to lost trust and faith in others and ourselves. This cuts women off from one of their most significant emotional resources. It is imperative that women resist the myths that socialize many to believe that women are incapable of true supportive sisterhood within friendship circles. These myths and internalizations can cause us to be competitive instead of compassionate and to seek out male approval instead of being comfortable approving of ourselves. It is important for women to seek out, create, and nurture their sisterhood network. We have to be intentional about honoring the time and effort required for a lasting successful friendship. We make time for the things that we honor most and we will do our best when we protect time for our sisters. Maintaining these positive connections requires communication skills, interpersonal skills, a level of vulnerability or willingness to share, and a commitment to the life of the friendship. Many of us may have been hurt or disappointed within past friendships but it is important not to generalize negative interactions with individuals to your view of women as friends in general. Our feelings about ourselves show up in how we treat all people, but particularly those who reflect our identity. To be a woman who doesn't like to be around other women is to be unhealthy. Given this issue I would recommend the following:

- Consider the things you need to work on within yourself so you can be a better sister friend.
- Select your sister friends based on matters of the heart not based on surface issues.
- Invest time and energy in developing and maintaining your connection with positive sister friends.

The presence of sister friends, like Edith, in our lives can enhance our well-being. The area of female friendships has been under-examined, particularly for African American women (Greif & Sharpe, 2010). Feminist psychologists recognize and prioritize this too often neglected area in their scholarship and practice. Feminist therapy seeks to empower women and the empowerment process includes the development of healthy relationships. It is healing to create opportunities within therapy and outside of therapy for women to be known, valued, and affirmed. It is when women are connected as sister friends that they can unite and mobilize to improve the lives of all women and girls. When women are isolated, it is hard for us to be agents of change. However, when we come together in meaningful ways we can be effective advocates for justice that reaches women of all walks of life. As womanist theorists have noted women-centered networks play an important role in assisting African American women to navigate oppressive, toxic environments by providing support, caretaking, spiritual guidance, and healthy constructions of the self (Williams & Wiggins, 2010). In short I have found in my personal and professional life that sister friends help us to survive and thrive. African American women's survival, health, and well-being must be our urgent platform (Banks-Wallace, 2000) and this requires a commitment to a sustained sisterhood.

REFERENCES

Andrews, J. O., Felton, G., Wewers, M., Waller, J., & Tingen, M. (2007). The effect of a multi-component smoking cessation intervention in African American women residing in public housing. *Research In Nursing & Health*, *30*(1), 45–60. doi:10.1002/nur.20174

Banks-Wallace, J. (2000). Womanist ways of knowing: Theoretical considerations for research with African American Women. *Advances In Nursing Science*, *22*(3), 33–45.

Bryant-Davis, T. (2005). Coping strategies of African American adult survivors of childhood violence. *Professional Psychology: Research And Practice*, *36*(4), 409–414. doi:10.1037/0735-7028.36.4.409

Bryant-Davis, T. (2005). *Thriving in the wake of trauma: A multicultural guide.* Westport, CT: Praeger Publishers/Greenwood Publishing Group.

Bryant-Davis, T., & Ocampo, C. (2006). A therapeutic approach to the treatment of racist-incident-based trauma. *Journal Of Emotional Abuse*, *6*(4), 1–22. doi:10.1300/J135v06n04_01

Day, A. (2004). The age thirty transition and social support: A qualitative examination of the age thirty transition experience for single professional African-American women. *Dissertation Abstracts International*, *64*.

Edwards, L. V. (2006). Perceived social support and HIV/AIDS medication adherence among African American women. *Qualitative Health Research*, *16*(5), 679–691. doi:10.1177/1049732305281597

Fries-Britt, S., & Kelly, B. (2005). Retaining each other: Narratives of two African American women in the academy. *The Urban Review*, *37*(3), 221–242. doi:10.1007/s11256-005-0006-2

Godfrey, J. E. (1997, July). Factors which influence the role of female friendships in the lives of heterosexual African-American women. *Dissertation Abstracts International, 58.*

Greif, G. L., & Sharpe, T. L. (2010). The friendships of women: Are there differences between African Americans and Whites? *Journal of Human Behavior In The Social Environment, 20*(6), 791–807. doi:10.1080/10911351003751892

Lincoln, K. D., Taylor, R. J., Chae, & Chatters, L. M. (2010). Demographic correlates of psychological well-being and distress among older Africans and Carribean black adults. *Best Practices in Mental Health: An International Journal, 6*(1), 103–126.

Person, T. (2005). Socialization experiences and friendships among African-American women. *Dissertation Abstracts International, 65.*

Samter, W., Whaley, B. B., Mortenson, S. T., & Burleson, B. R. (1997). Ethnicity and emotional support in same-sex friendship: A comparison of Asian-Americans, African-Americans, and Euro-Americans. *Personal Relationships, 4*(4), 413–430. doi:10.1111/j.1475-6811.1997.tb00154.x

Shaw, K. M., & Coleman, A. B. (2000). Humble on Sundays: Family, friends, and faculty in the upward mobility experiences of African American females. *Anthropology & Education Quarterly, 31*(4), 449–470. doi:10.1525/aeq.2000.31.4.449.

Shorter-Gooden, K. (2004). Multiple resistance strategies: How African American women cope with racism and sexism. *Journal of Black Psychology, 30*(3), 406–425. doi:10.1177/0095798404266050

Simoni, J. M., Huang, B., Goodry, E. J., & Montoya, H. D. (2005). Social support and depressive symptomatology among HIV-positive women: The mediating role of self-esteem and mastery. *Women & Health, 42*(4), 1–15. doi:10.1300/J013v42n04_01

Washington, O. M., Moxley, D. P., & Garriott, L. (2009). The telling my story quilting workshop: Innovative group work with older African American women transitioning out of homelessness. *Journal of Psychosocial Nursing And Mental Health Services, 47*(11), 42–52. doi:10.3928/02793695-20090930-01

Williams, C. (2005). Counseling African American women: Multiple identities—multiple constraints. *Journal of Counseling & Development, 83*(3), 278–283. doi:10.1002/j.1556-6678.2005.tb00343.x

Williams, C., & Wiggins, M. I. (2010). Womanist spirituality as a response to the racism-sexism double bind in African American women. *Counseling and Values, 54*(2), 17–186.

Awakening Resilience: Recovery Within Intimate Female Friendships

IVA GREYWOLF

University of Alaska Fairbanks College of Rural & Community Development, Fairbanks, Alaska; University of Alaska Southeast, Sitka, Alaska

A multi-ethnic female creates her own definition of self with the help of strong female role models—women of strength. The author uses a storytelling method, characteristic Native American way of relating, as a vehicle for her narration. It is a story of transitions with challenges in relationships and new beginnings that define the woman as well as the therapist.

From birth I've been alone yet not alone. Being a mixed blood Indian on a reservation in the 1950s was not easy. To make the situation more difficult, I had a light complexion and light hair. There was not an easy fit with the Indians or the non-Indians. I learned to be alone. I learned to observe, to listen. This was the beginning of my path to define myself.

When I was little, my grandmother Wolf told each of her grandchildren stories. Each child had their own unique story and we heard our stories over and over. Mine was the Ugly Duckling. Of course I wanted a different fairytale or a different legend. Although I wanted a different story to be mine, my grandmother patiently told the story to me again and again. I compared my story with the stories of the other grandchildren. Initially it befuddled me. It took me a long while to understand my grandmother's wisdom. When I finally understood it was okay to be different and that I still had value, there was a transformation. It was the first notable transformation in my life that I recall. My grandmother taught me about my innate beauty in her own indirect way. Through her patience and repetition she was a woman of influence in my life.

In those early years I experienced poverty and violence not uncommon in the reservation environment. As hard as my road was, it was more difficult to see my sisters and others with darker complexions mistreated by teachers, other students and business owners. The opportunities for "growth" were many. My survival skills were honed and my heart of compassion was growing.

Who do I marvel at? Who has inspired me? Who has supported me? Who has challenged me? These are the female relationships that I'm going to write about. Each of these relationships has had a powerful influence in my life. Like so many other women of strength, I have had a multitude of supporters, most of them female.

As a child, I needed someone to look up to. The strength of my grandmothers rooted me. They raised many children under difficult conditions. Through all of the challenges they remained dignified. Some of the circumstances they could not change but they had control of their attitudes, beliefs and conduct. Perhaps this is the essence of "carrying oneself well when things are not going so well" (a Yupik teaching). They displayed high moral standards and a strong work ethic and were not afraid to own their power. Their power was evident in their physical presence, in their words. One used fewer words than the other and her presence was more potent. Where did their power stem from? Was it from their spiritual path or simply their tenacious natures? Perhaps the answer contains elements of both. Whatever it was it resulted in them being comfortable in their own skins. They did not need to be different than what they were. They loved and they were loved. What more can a young girl ask than to have strong women in her family circle? I was poor but rich.

One of my strong friendships ended up being with my mother's best friend from youth. Their paths went different directions as time passed. My mother moved far away. As a young adult, I moved back to my mother's hometown and somehow became a spiritual prayer partner with my mother's best friend from high school, Genevieve Bergie. She did not have an education beyond high school. She was a strong practicing Catholic and I was involved in traditional Indian spiritual practices. Indeed, American Indian women are spiritual people (Weahkee, 2008). Together we shared a deep respect for each other's path and had regular and powerful prayer sessions. We read the Bible. I sometimes attended her church and she sometimes attended traditional ceremonies. She firmly believed in the power of prayer and she supported me in her unique way.

Her loyalty was strong. She could offer me another perspective that I was blind to and I could do the same for her. We could cry with one another and we could laugh with one another. Despite our age differences, our bond was strong. I learned from her to be present with intensity and not to avoid difficulties.

Role models for a mixed blood Indian female were few and far between in professional circles. When I was younger I was clearer about my professional strengths. Age has softened my high estimation of myself. In rural/remote areas where I lived and worked, there were no Indian female psychologists. There was one across the state but I did not have regular access to her as a colleague. There were other Indian female professionals in fields outside of psychology in my community. There were a couple of non-Indian female psychologists that I had access to. The lack of professional role models that I had likely contributed to my determination to complete my education.

When I began graduate school, I found others similar to me. A classmate in my Master's program shared my journey. She was involved in substance abuse as I had been. She had also experienced sexual assault as I had—as well as many other Native American women have experienced (Amnesty International, 2007). She was intelligent and had a mindset that would not allow her to take the stance of a victim. Debbie taught me to reframe every assault on my person through a lens of strength. No matter what the situation, even cancer, she refused to perceive herself as a victim. She defined herself as a strong Indian woman.

I learned from her to operate from a position of strength, to be fiercely honest with myself, and to recognize different paths to a healthy place. Such a mindset is consistent with feminist therapy's principle of rescuing women's strengths for empowerment (Worell & Johnson, 1997). We each chose different ways to embrace healthy lifestyles. Our comfort is so great; we pick up where we left off even after years of separation. Each new conversation is an invigorating new examination of life experiences. I respect her. I value her contributions. She inspires me as a healthy Indian woman.

My return to graduate school gave me more friends on a similar journey. A classmate and I became good friends. We shared many hard experiences together. Because we were both minority students, we both had children and our financial and academic challenges were many. I felt obliged to support her as we worked toward our degrees. My children told me I helped too much but I did not recognize that. I told myself if we can't help one another, what are we doing in this field?

I did not recognize my own codependent nature at that time. As time has allowed me to reflect on the events I recognize there was not mutual give-and-take. I was meeting my own need by being the "savior" for my friend. She allowed me to make it easy for her. She was having a hard enough time with a lost romance on top of the other challenges. I was blind to being taken advantage of. We were at a younger time in our lives where we valued what others thought too much, bought into society's standards for what is beautiful, what a heterosexual woman should do, what is a romantic relationship, and the importance of a male in our lives. We did all of this on top of facing the rigors of graduate school. My priorities at that time were askew.

Our naïve acceptance of what the media was promoting about beauty and love was all too common. Fortunately, the women's liberation movement was alive and well and eventually came to our rural environment. Although it was a struggle I could see holes in the media's false presentations of women and love. At that time I also was working with females who had been sexually abused. My grandmothers' rules of propriety began to ring true.

One client—in particular—had been sexually abused by her father. She had known a significant amount of trauma. Like many clients with similar histories, she indiscriminately accepted what was presented in the media and she had an unrealistically positive view of her counselor's life. It wasn't until many years later I found out she had an affair with my husband. How sad for all of us. She chased the mirage of her desire, attempted to hold it and found out it was insubstantial.

As I proceeded through graduate school, my husband struggled with the reality of his wife getting a PhD. He was not comfortable with the change of events even though he had supported the process. Insecurities ran amok. Fate intervened and I was hit hard with a debilitating illness. All of my energy had to focus on just getting through the day. A friend of mine and my husband were drawn to each other during this time. My family witnessed what was happening and brought this to my attention.

Truly women in my life have promoted my growth through love, laughter and betrayal. For me, deep betrayal could only come from the ones closest to me that I had a relationship with. There were women outside my circle of friends involved with my husband, like my client, yet the deepest pain came from those I shared my secrets and laughter with. These women became my teachers; teachers that made me stretch.

My marriage ended not due to the betrayals but to other factors. My friendship cooled I took the time to focus on my own growth and heal. The combination of factors pushed me to engage in my own therapy. I mourned the loss of what never really was and examined the illusion. I came to accept their humanness and mine. Because of them my heart of compassion has grown. Such as it was, we were all doing the best we could do under the circumstances. I can be a friend again on a more equal level and I can embrace love and live again more fully.

Forgiving myself and forgiving others has freed me to see life as it is not as I want to be. The healing journey took me back to my traditional practices where I gained clarity and insight. Breaking through the fictitious messages presented in our society is challenging. It takes hard work and far too many individuals would rather avoid that or chase the fantasy. Should they be judged? I think not. My experience has shown me many people do not even recognize the source of their discomfort. Being a feminist therapist has helped me to engage in a process of woman-valuing and validating not only my experience but also those of other women (Brown, 2010; Lerman, 1986).

Many women have been socialized not to stop and analyze internal qualities and external experiences that are truly important to them. Without this clarity the experience of living is through a hazy lens.

Some women break free through the haze and engage in broadminded analyses. Independent thinking impresses me and independent women continue to amaze me. Through them I am reminded to challenge myself. Paraphrasing Neale Donald Walsch, (http://www.goodreads.com/quotes/show/10646), I remember that Life begins at the end of [my] comfort zone. A current colleague of mine, Beth Kersey, has an impressive expanse of interests. Her education has crossed international boundaries. She is a prolific writer and a comprehensive thinker who continuously stimulates my thinking and therefore my growth. The breadth and depth of her thinking makes me smile. My mind sees her grabbing life with both hands and holding on for the ride!

For each of these powerful women in my life I am grateful. I have shared moments of love and laughter with each of them. They helped me become comfortable in my own skin. From these relationships I have grown as a therapist and as a healthy role model. Humanness, humor, generosity, compassion, and individual growth were all part of the relationships and are also part of the therapeutic work I engage in. Each of these women has offered me a view of another facet in the spectrum of life. Some of the experiences I liked better than others yet I know each of the experiences have allowed me to become who I am today.

The strong memories of betrayal are seared into my memory. The resolution brings me peace and allows me to let others know from a heartfelt position that healing can take place. I can still see the beauty of others even when they have harmed me. Healing is not quick nor is it easy. Fervent honesty and persistence and little steps eventually lead to accomplishing the goal. It is only through the adversity that wisdom is obtained.

LESSONS LEARNED

"If you are going through hell, keep going."

– Winston Churchill

My healing took place a long time ago. As with many women in pain, I did not seek out psychology articles or psychology texts to help me through that experience. However, I can recall hearing a presenter, Robin Casarjian, who spoke about freedom through forgiveness. She was working with incarcerated populations with a forgiveness curriculum and the healing work was very powerful. I became interested in her work and read her book "Houses of Healing" (Casarjian, 1995). This volume certainly had a positive impact on my healing.

At that time I was also heavily involved in learning about co-dependency (Beattie, 1992) and the impact of alcoholism on families. However, the most important part of my healing experience was participating in traditional healing ceremonies. Actually, getting out of my "head" and focusing on my "heart" was necessary for me to heal. I don't think I wanted to feel anymore. A quote that resonated with me is, "If you are going through hell, keep going." I don't think I could concentrate very well (especially to read) while in pain; I needed the physical demands and ritual to ground me. I needed to witness the experiences of others to reframe my own experience.

CONCLUSION

My most meaningful professional work is with those who are not yet awake to life. They move through their life but don't truly live in their bodies. What wakes them up? For many, it is having a witness as they walk through their pain at the same time showing them by example that one can live with their eyes wide open.

Proof that the Creator cares for me: I was reading "The Dance of Deception" by Harriet G. Lerner (1993) when my family confronted me with my husband's history of infidelity.

REFERENCES

Amnesty International (2007). Maze of injustice: The failure to protect indigenous women from sexual abuse in the U.S.A. Retrieved on May 15, 2012 from https://docs.google.com/viewer?a=v&q=cache:j8a8YpNcMLoJ:www.amnestyusa.org/pdfs/MazeOfInjustice.pdf+&hl=en&gl=us&pid=bl&srcid=ADGEESgsA4-a9vwzlCpzinu75zddLICEcbN0w6YwOae0fHp36Ndy-IYlqSgJKH3yj_EVCFs_FA7v_5G-3Ak0o8HlcbTf-RXYfLV4Y4OO1FVEWR46LStUurkHjhXDvFTJHFDi5GUA-w3h&sig=AHIEtbR0thAwOuVmwwh_ViL_s06oBuXWhw&pli=1

Beattie, M. (1992). *Codependent no more: How to stop controlling others and start caring for yourself.* Center City, MN: Hazelden Foundation.

Brown, L. S. (2010). *Feminist therapy*. Theories of Psychotherapy Series. Washington, DC: American Psychological Association

Casarjian, R. (1995). *Houses of healing: A prisoner's guide to inner power and freedom.* Boston: The Lionheart Foundation.

Lerman, 1H. (1986). *A mote in Freud's eye: From psychoanalysis to the psychology of women.* New York: Springer.

Lerner, H. G. (1993). *The dance of deception: A guide to authenticity and truth-telling in women's relationships.* New York: Harper Collins Publishers.

Weahkee, R. L. (2008). American Indian women and spirituality. In C. Raybrun & L. Comas-Diaz (Eds.), *WomanSoul: The inner life of women's spirituality* (pp. 107–118). Westport, CT: Praeger.

Worrell, J., & Johnson, N. G. (Eds.), (1997). *Shaping the future of feminist psychology: Education, research, and practice.* Washington, DC: American Psychological Association.

Make New Friends but Keep the Old: The Sisterhood Bonds that Have Shaped Me

MICHI FU

California School of Professional Psychology of Alliant International University and Asian Pacific Family Center of Pacific Clinics, Los Angeles, California

The relationships in an Asian American psychologist's life have helped to shape her as a person as well as a professional. Specifically, a review of significant female relationships indicates that they have contributed to the author's therapeutic style. In this article, the author explores some of the relationships with other women in her life and illustrates how they have informed her role as a therapist. She concludes with a case vignette illustrating how some of these concepts were applied to a long-term therapy client.

> "Have you heard of the ugly duckling?" Selina, my middle-school tutor, asked.
> "No," I dumbly replied.
> "You are like the ugly duckling ... waiting to blossom into a beautiful swan. You just don't know it yet."

It was the first time I can recall allowing myself to see the potential that someone else saw in me. Up until this point, my curiosity oftentimes earned me the nickname of "troublemaker" among the adults at home. If something was broken, chances were likely that it was because my inquisitiveness got the best

The author would like to especially thank Dr. Lillian Comas-Diaz for her support of this manuscript and Ms. Kaitlyn Masai for her personal contribution of the supporting literature for this article.

of me and I *had* to figure out how something could be taken apart, where doors led to or what happened when certain buttons were depressed. Needless to say, I became accustomed to exasperated adults' attempts to tame me.

Looking back, I can see how fortunate I was to have a mentor that ferociously sought to help me see something that I could not see in myself. She fought for me to channel my energy into a productive path. Over the next decade and beyond, Selina and I developed a relationship from tutor/tutee to something that resembled family. I wouldn't know when I met her that I'd spend countless holidays with her and eventually be her maid-of-honor on one of the most important days of her life.

> It was she that asked me: "What do you want to be when you grow up?"
> "A waitress!" the 12-year-old me answered enthusiastically.
> "Give me three reasons why you want to become a waitress," she patiently responded.
> "One, I would get to help people, two, no two days would ever be the same, and three, I could earn tips and food."
> "What if we were to take those reasons and find other jobs that you could also be good at?"

Thus, Selina helped to shape my career as a child psychologist, by applying the same reasons: (1) caring profession, (2) flexibility and variety in daily routine and (3) an ability to sustain myself.

This article will offer a reflection of how significant female relationships have helped to form who I am as a woman and as a professional. I will explore how some of these relationships have informed my approach to my teaching and therapeutic approaches.

YA-TOU (MANDARIN CHINESE FOR "USELESS GIRL"—A TERM OF ENDEARMENT)

Starting this manuscript has been a challenge. Upon reflecting on the important female relationships in my life, I became emotional as I thought of those who helped to shape who I am today. These "sisters" have helped me survive my ugly duckling (Hans, 1844) phase and remind me of the swan they see when I have difficulty envisioning her.

I grew up in a traditional, Confucian-based family where males were prized. In such households where Confucian values are upheld, "good" females are expected to be passive, subservient and docile throughout their lifetime (Kawahara & Fu, 2007). For example, the Law of Three Obediences dictates that a female is supposed to obey (1) her father as a daughter, (2) her husband as an adult and (3) her oldest son in her older age. This was a fortunate position for my brother, who was the only boy of the oldest son (my father) of an only son (my grandfather). I was told at a young age that my parents were initially ambivalent about being pregnant with me when they discovered they were to have another girl. I tried hard to be the boy that my parents might have cherished, but learning kung-fu and riding dirt bikes with my brother could not change that I was born a female. Like many other women before me, I had been socialized to devalue my own gender (Stewart & McDermott, 2004). I battled my parents' expectations of how a "good daughter" should behave (e.g., "How are we supposed to marry you off if you don't learn your way around the kitchen?") until they eventually began to acknowledge the value of the daughters that they had raised. Growing up, it's no wonder that I devalued relationships with many same-sex peers and adults. I had learned that the female perspective was dismissible and therefore prided myself in being a neighborhood tomboy.

SISTERS HANAI (HAWAIIAN FOR "FOSTER/ADOPT")

Despite growing up in a household that taught me the feminine is to be discounted, one of the earliest bonds I developed was with my Girl Scout Troop. I developed social skills that were invaluable. The camping trips forced me to develop survival skills, selling calendars taught me how to engage with others, the plethora of field trips exposed me to extracurricular activities that my immigrant family may not have valued as readily. Most importantly, I learned the value of being part of an all-female tribe. We learned how to rely on one another as a social network and I am forever grateful to Mrs. Zahm for having the patience to shepherd our troop for as long as she did. To this day, I credit Girl Scouts for teaching me to respect others, the environment, and myself. This sense of empowerment is something that I try and relay to my clients during therapy (Enns, 1997).

Female classmates and colleagues throughout my educational/professional career have made a difference in the person I am today. Certainly, girl scouts shaped my sense of responsibility and gave me the confidence I needed to sell cookies and ideas later on in life. My college roommates, Janet and Sandy, were there to witness many of my coming of age experiences. The innocence and faith that we shared were priceless. Elaine and Kathleen adopted me into the Three Musketeers and helped me to survive the coldness of Boston by role modeling ways to nurture ourselves (Singh & Burnes, 2011) with countless study sessions that included homemade vodka penne, discount-bin bottles of Beaujolais, and belly laughs. Malou's companionship extended beyond grad school and taught me that forgiving relationships can survive men, geography, and time. Irene and Rowena showed me how to respect and celebrate differences (Enns, 1997). Iris educates me on how to express and receive love languages.

Gal pals I've been fortunate enough to meet through other avenues in my life have also taught me important lessons. TsuAnn exemplifies being civic-minded and sacrificing for one's beliefs. Grayce shows how to stand up for what one believes in. Brenda helps me to be playful and curious. Vicky inspires me to see more of the world. Ching demonstrates unconditional loyalty. Mauie shows the importance of striking a work-life balance. Joyce encourages me to appreciate and explore the arts. Myrtle role models how to engage in self-care throughout the lifespan.

STANDING ON THE SHOULDERS OF GIANTS

My role models have been extremely generous by helping me to see the potential that I couldn't always see in myself. Selina, my first mentor, gave me the confidence I needed to attend my first dance and strike a career path. Kathy Davis, our high school music teacher, gave me a chance to shine on stage and sing from my heart by hand-picking me for the school musical and the prestigious Jazz Singers. Tammy, a professor from my doctoral studies, offered me opportunities to work with her. She also nurtured my sense of spirituality when I didn't know how to integrate this aspect of myself with my professional identity by sharing tools with me, such as the labyrinth. Allyson, my internship training director, gave me a sense of family and accepted my far-fetched ideas by helping to see them to fruition. Evie, the epitome of a fair supervisor, encouraged us to maintain a sense of humor while maintaining our professional responsibilities. Kumea, my poised role model for how to be a strong female of color, taught me how to be graceful and diplomatic. Beth, my colleague, leads with integrity and warmly encourages me to be the most ethical supervisor I can be. Each of these role models have taught me how to be a better educator and trainer for those students, assistants, or trainees that I have had the privilege of working with. I strive to work openly with and empathically nurture the potential in those that I work with in a fashion that mimics those upon whose shoulders I stand.

THE WIND BENEATH MY WINGS

My family is my heart and soul. Without them, I have no roots and life would seem meaningless. My cousins and aunts give me a sense of history and have taught me to enjoy indulgences of life. Hot springs, afternoon teas and shopping sprees were bonding rituals for the women in my family. My siblings demonstrate that love includes daily selfless sacrifices, oftentimes finding happiness when their generosity is bestowed upon their loved ones. My Grandmother Li showed me the power of uncompromising wisdom. My mother teaches me how perseverance and dedication can result in reaching seemingly insurmountable goals. I will spend the remainder of this journal reflecting upon the impact of various female family members.

My Belle

My sister is a fragile flower. Growing up, she was always the beautiful and fearless oldest grandchild who made everyone laugh and follow her lead. She excelled in languages and had an amazing sense of wit and fashion. I recall times when she would orchestrate elaborate theatrical productions in our living room. Though she could have capitalized on her external beauty, she opted to graduate from college and passed the state exam to be an educator. She had her share of suitors and chose her marriage partner wisely, giving birth to my two wonderful nephews.

I was shocked and felt helpless when she began to experience postpartum complications leading to frantic phone calls from my parents asking me how to help her regain her mental well-being. Our family was in denial for years that she had a serious mental illness that could be effectively treated through the attention of mental health professionals. Instead, she spent months in confinement or on various holistic healing regimens that would inevitably fall short. My dear sister taught me how to have compassion and true empathy for those suffering from severe mental illnesses. Hers is a textbook case of exhausting spiritual, holistic, etc. healing options. Her situation is also a classic example of Asians presenting as more severe than the average population, due to use of mental health treatment as a last resort, whereby underutilization of mental health services doesn't necessarily indicate a lack of need, but instead reflects a reluctance to utilize such services (Yang & WonPat-Borja, 2007). Fortunately, she had enough resilience and social supports to assist in her recovery process. It is because of her journey that I have a zealous belief that Asians can receive help if they are served in a culturally appropriate manner, which includes enlisting the aide of family members and working collaboratively with other healers. Therefore, she has taught me the power of working within a system. I've also seen how spirituality, art, and working with her bicultural background have been integral elements in her recovery—all influencing my own style of helping others.

A Life Worth Living

My Grandmother Li was a young widow when my grandfather left her with eight children to raise. Equipped with a high school diploma, she was resourceful and passed away with over a hundred direct descendants just a year shy of being a centurion. I'm told she was strict with her children, but all I can recall is being in awe of my beloved grandmother's timeless insight, incredible wit, infectious sense of humor, and passion for life. She was a vegetarian well before it was trendy so that she would live a healthy life. When we were younger, I recall whining to keep up with her energetic pace while hiking in the mountains of Taiwan: "A-ma, please slow down. You're going too fast." When she eventually became confined to her wheelchair, she channeled her energy into completing more studies and satiated her need for social connection by arranging for daily visitors to accompany her. When it became too cumbersome to entertain others in the common sitting areas, she kept her mind active through meditation and chanting, drawing and coloring pictures, and speaking with each of her children (each of whom she had pre-programmed as speed dial numbers on the large buttons of her telephone). She's the epitome of one who is able to reframe and make the most out of a seemingly dismal situation. My Grandmother Li reminds me of the power of positive psychology, spirituality, and the role that art can have in maintaining well-being.

Ma (Taiwanese for "Mother")

I am both proud and fearful of the woman who gave me birth. According to the Zodiac calendar, she is born the year of the Oxen (as am I). The typical Ox is described to be persevering, intellectually astute, and determined. She was the youngest of eight children and the oftentimes described as a charming beauty while growing up. When someone says "no" to my mother, she usually hears "Try another method and I *might* be persuaded." This means that she's managed to convince (1) airlines to hold the flight for us when we are running late for a family trip, (2) school administrators to reconsider admission decisions for her children and (3) people to donate significant resources to causes that she believes in. What's even more amazing is that she has an ability to make others believe that it was their idea in the first place and to *thank* her for the opportunity. After my father passed away, I feared that she would wander aimlessly without a purpose. Much to the contrary, she became volunteer extraordinaire at her temple and finds that she is in even higher demand in various social and civic circles.

Rarely have I yelled at anyone at the top of my lungs, yet I'm not proud to say that my relationship with my mother used to bring out this side of me. Chua's (2011) description of the "Tiger mother" reminded me of my own upbringing so much that a part of me was somewhat validated to see in print that a mother may truly believe that loving one's offspring can sometimes be expressed in the strict Eastern parenting style that Chua described in her book. Simply stated, this method of parenting includes (1) expecting uncompromising excellence rather than mediocrity, (2) shapes behavior through offering critical feedback rather than reinforcement/praise, and (3) is based on Confucian concepts such as saving face and following hierarchical order. Growing up, I fantasized that my misfortune for being raised with such an unrelenting parenting style must have been a mistake. I now know that my mother based her decisions and behaviors on love and convictions. Perhaps being faced with mortality issues have helped us both to listen to one another more effectively, since nowadays I spend more time trying to learn from and listen to my Oxen mother. Or, perhaps I have become more open to her as she approaches me with a new softness in her older age. Whatever the case may be, I am now experiencing her love for me in a way that lets me know she values me as a "good" daughter.

My mother's influence on my professional work has been undeniable. The recapitulation of our cycle of cultural conflicts and resolutions has led me to help other immigrant families with their bicultural conflicts. She has also taught me the value of working effectively with power dynamics, family systems, holistic healing, and spirituality. Thanks to my parents for feigning English incompetence with their children in an effort to keep language from our cultural background spoken in the home, I am now able to conduct therapy sessions in conversational Taiwanese and Mandarin. I've learned to cherish being bicultural and use this in my professional contacts with clients and consulting endeavors.

MY IDENTITY AS A TAIWANESE-AMERICAN PSYCHOLOGIST

As a professional, it's sometimes difficult to quantify what I do for a living. I feel very fortunate to belong to a profession that gives me pride while continuing to make me feel fulfilled. As it turns out, I have chosen a profession that is highly congruent with my own personal mission statement (which I encourage people to revisit at least annually to maximize personal life satisfaction). It would seem that there are a few aspects of my professional identity that may distinguish me from other colleagues. To summarize, there are elements that I incorporate into my professional work that have been influenced by the significant female relationships in my life:

- Art therapy
- Play therapy
- Meditation
- Holistic healing
- Systems/Bowenian
- Bicultural identity/Bilingual therapy
- Power dynamics
- Cultural conflict/Multicultural
- Spirituality
- Advocacy (social justice)
- Mentor
- Work-life balance
- Person-centered therapy
- Existential work
- Mindfulness
- Positive psychology

It's difficult to describe how these elements all come together without anchoring these parts of my professional identity into an actual example of how I work. Therefore, I'll proceed to illustrate my style as a therapist through my work with a trauma survivor.

SWEET CAROLINE: A CASE STUDY

Caroline (pseudonym used to protect the identity of an actual client) was a 39-year-old multiracial (Hawaiian, Chinese and Filipino) female when I was assigned as her therapist at a sex and trauma center. She was mandated for therapy after child welfare services removed her children for neglect. Presenting symptoms indicated Post-Traumatic Stress Disorder (PTSD) related to her own childhood history of molestation and domestic violence, which was recently triggered by a series of prolonged and violent rape episodes at the hands of her sadistic captor. It's no wonder that she found relief in occasionally abusing substances. She had already deemed counseling services in the past to be ineffective and was therefore initially skeptical of this therapist. I knew at the onset of our three-year relationship that my initial task would be to gain her trust.

Interventions that we used during Caroline's treatment included: art therapy, group therapy, sand tray therapy, person-centered therapy, couples/family therapy, spirituality/prayer, holistic healing, cultural adaptation of treatment and advocacy. When we began to work together, Caroline made it clear that she didn't think talking could help return her children. I had to spend some time negotiating the power dynamics between us. She was older than I was and had life experiences she didn't think I could relate to (e.g., having multiple children and being an incest survivor). Additionally, my education and professional position created distance between us. I needed to address our relationship structure (Enns, 1997) before we could make any significant progress. I learned early on in our relationship that I'd need to engage in self-disclosures and self-involving responses (Remer, 2012) so that she would experience me as genuine.

Rather than engage her in talk therapy, I asked her to simply draw for me. Art therapy opened her up in a non-defensive way (Foster & Viney, 2007; Hughes, 2010). She drew what she thought of her body before her stepfather forced himself on her. We also incorporated sand tray therapy so that she could develop themes of trauma and eventually rehearse feelings of safety (Fitzpatrick, 2001). When she was ready to, we would incorporate dance/movement into our sessions so that she could reclaim her body (Leseho & Maxwell, 2010).

Though the majority of her treatment involved individual therapy sessions, it became clear that she needed support in order for her to improve significantly. I invited her partner to occasionally participate as a collateral contact for her individual sessions and pave the way for couples counseling or family therapy (Harvard Mental Health Letter, 2009; Schwartz, 2001).

Inviting her to work with others created a possibility for her to engage in group therapy with other women who had experienced similar traumas. The Adults Molested As Children (AMAC) group was geared towards empowering females, leading to targeted symptom reduction (Greenfield, Cummings, & Gallop, 2010; Wechsberg, Lam, Zule, & Bobashev, 2004). Group members shared collages depicting their lives pre- and post-molestation, focusing on nonverbal emotional expression and validation through shared experiences (Erickson & Young, 2010). Hers was the type of upbringing where she hadn't learned how to be a child and play. Thus, a byproduct of participating in the AMAC group was to provide her a safe space to access her inner child through play (Yarnal, 2006).

Eventually, she came to trust me and took the lead in sharing her trauma her-story with me verbally. Developing intimate female relationships was foreign to her and therefore our relationship was oftentimes precarious. I summoned all of the person-centered empathy I could in order to withstand her frequent accusations that I couldn't possibly understand or care for her. This may have been due in part to her having the type of mother to deny that her second husband could molest her daughter and furthermore insinuate that Caroline seduced her stepfather (her mother's second husband). Therefore, I understood that a critical part of my role as her therapist was to also deal with possible transference issues she had towards members of her own gender (Flemke, 2001).

When she began to open up more about the ineffective coping strategies she had developed (e.g., unhealthy relationships, substance abuse, and self-mutilation), she relayed a readiness to improve the way she had learned to deal with her stressors and pain. The list of things that she created which tended to help her feel better included being outdoors and reconnecting with her sense of spirituality (Berrett, Hardman, O'Grady, & Richards, 2007). I still recall the first time she asked if I would pray with her—as if she were making a phone call to a long-lost relative. I was aware of the need to culturally modify what I had learned about Western psychotherapy in order to meet her needs as a mixed-race female who embraced an indigenous perspective regarding spirituality and incorporating healers from other disciplines. She realized her addiction to substances wouldn't be easily addressed and was therefore amenable to working closely with holistic healers that could help with her urges to use. Finally, my role as her advocate was central in convincing child protective services of the progress that she had made, ultimately leading to an arduous but successful road towards family reunification.

I am fortunate to have had the opportunity to work intimately with Caroline given that her initial prognosis seemed challenging at best. However, she taught me much about how to incorporate the various skills I'd acquired when the client is ready. I was privileged enough to see how her timid drawings at the onset of therapy blossomed into angry poetry in the middle of treatment and eventually morphed into healing dance movements. I owe the progress she was able to make to the female relationships in my own life, which have helped to shape my approach to working with others. My sense of play, willingness to use creative methods, openness towards incorporating spirituality and other methods of healing, ability to sit with another, obligation to advocate for others, etc. have all been passed onto me by the sisters of my heart.

ZEST FOR LIFE

The risk of vicarious traumatization for psychologists makes self-care all the more important. In order to write this article, I needed to reflect upon who I am as a professional and a person. As it turns out, the two are highly related to one another. My personal philosophy in life is to "work hard, play harder." I am fortunate to have gal pals in my life who are living examples that having a successful career doesn't mean one has to give up a fabulous personal life. Ching, an artist, reminds me to take care of myself in order to take care of others. Ji, my college roommate, has always been a good sport about letting me play restaurant roulette so that we can try out the menu of the latest hotspots. When I want to learn a new dance, I can always count on Vicky, a fellow psychologist, to help me pick out the right shoes and teach me the most difficult moves. When I've needed to stare at mind-bending art, Brenda, an independent consultant, has patiently helped me to decipher the possible meanings behind the artists' intentions. TsuAnn, a university administrator, spoils me with visits to her private retreat. Grayce, a community organizer, knows exactly when I need to sing karaoke without a care in the world. Myrtle, a retired educator turned psychologist, reminds me that we can stay forever young as long as we remain open to learning. My wanderlust ways were most likely inherited by my family and are fortunately supported by girlfriends who serve as willing travel companions during the holidays and such. Without them, I wouldn't have had female companionship during the elephant ride in Thailand, the hike up the Pantheon, or star-gazing in Sedona. In short, I have my friends and family to thank for supporting my zest for life and keeping me balanced.

REFLECTIONS

Girl Scout Troop 228 ended each of our meetings holding hands and singing: "Make new friends but keep the old. One is silver and the other gold." I can now see that I kept these words close to my heart for the sisters of my heart are truly precious to me and have helped to shape the healer and advocate that I have become for others.

REFERENCES

Anderson, H. C. (1844). *The ugly duckling*, http://hca.gilead.org.il/ugly_duc.html.

Berrett, M. E., Hardman, R. K., O'Grady, K. A., & Richards, P. (2007). The Role of spirituality in the treatment of trauma and eating disorders: Recommendations for clinical practice. *Eating Disorders, 15*(4), 373–389. doi:10.1080/10640260701454394

Chua, A. (2011). *Battle hymn of the tiger mother.* New York: The Penguin Press.

Enns, C. Z. (1997). *Feminist theories and feminist psychotherapies: Origins, themes, and variations*. Binghamton, NY: Harrington Park Press.

Erickson, B. J., & Young, M. E. (2010). Group art therapy with incarcerated women. *Journal Of Addictions & Offender Counseling, 31*(1), 38–51.

Fitzpatrick, J. G. (2001). Sandplay and women's spirituality. *Women & Therapy, 24*(3-4), 161–173. doi:10.1300/J015v24n03_10

Flemke, K. R. (2001). The marginalization of intimate friendship between women within the context of therapy. *Journal Of Feminist Family Therapy, 13*(1), 75–91.

Foster, H., & Viney, L. L. (2007). Nonverbal explorations of construing: Drawing menopause. *Journal Of Constructivist Psychology, 20*(2), 147–165. doi:10.1080/10720530601074705

http://www.girlscouts.org/for_adults/leader_magazine/2004_springsing_along_with_us.asp

Greenfield, S. F., Cummings, S. M., & Gallop, R. J. (2010). Self-efficacy and substance use outcomes for women in single-gender versus mixed-gender group treatment. *Journal of Groups in Addition & Recovery, 5*(1), 4–16.

Hughes, E. (2010). Art therapy as a healing tool for sub-fertile women. *Journal Of Medical Humanities, 31*(1), 27–36. doi:10.1007/s10912-009-9098-0

Kawahara, D. M. & Fu, M. (2007). The psychology and mental health of Asian American women. In F. T. L. Leong, A. G. Inman, A. Ebreo, L. H. Yang, L. Kinoshita, & M. Fu (Eds.), *Handbook of Asian American psychology* (2nd ed.), (pp. 181–196). Thousand Oaks, CA: Sage.

Krasner, M. (2004). Mindfulness-based interventions: A coming of age? *Families, Systems & Health: The Journal Of Collaborative Family Healthcare, 22*(2), 207–212.

Leseho, J., & Maxwell, L. (2010). Coming alive: Creative movement as a personal coping strategy on the path to healing and growth. *British Journal Of Guidance & Counselling, 38*(1), 17–30. doi:10.1080/03069880903411301

Remer, P. (2012). Feminist therapy. In J. Frew & M. D. Spiegler (Eds.), *Contemporary psychotherapies for a diverse world* (pp. 373–414). New York: Routledge.

Schwartz, L. B. (2001). Family systems discourse: Conversations with clients concerning the impact of family legacies upon sexual desire. *Journal Of Sex & Marital Therapy, 27*(5), 603–606.

Singh, A. A., & Burnes, T. R. (2011). Feminist therapy and street-level activism: Revisiting our roots and "acting up" in the next decade. *Women & Therapy, 34*(1), 129–142.

Stewart, A. J., & McDermott, C. (2004). Gender in psychology. *Annual Review of Psychology, 55*, 519–544.

Treating bulimia nervosa. (2009). *Harvard Mental Health Letter, 26*(3), 4-5.

Wechsberg, W. M., Lam, W. K., Zule, W. A., & Bobashev, G. (2004). Efficacy of a woman-focused intervention to reduce HIV risk and increase self-sufficiency among African American crack abusers. *American Journal Of Public Health*, *94*(7), 1165–1173.

Yang, L. H., & WonPat-Borja, A. J. (2007). Psychopathology among Asian Americans. In F. T. L. Leong, A. G. Inman, A. Ebreo, L. H. Yang, L. Kinoshita, & M. Fu (Eds.), *Handbook of Asian American psychology* (2nd ed.) (pp. 379–405). Thousand Oaks, CA: Sage.

Yarnal, C. (2006). The red hat society: Exploring the role of play, liminality, and communitas in older women's lives. *Journal of Women & Aging*, *18*(3), 51–73. doi:10.1300/J074v18n03_05

Conclusion: SisterHeart: How Intimate Friendships Empower and Transform Women

LILLIAN COMAS-DIAZ

Transcultural Mental Health Institute, Washington, DC

Female friendships that work are relationships in which women help each other to belong to themselves.
– Louise Bernikow

INTRODUCTION

Our longing for intimate women friends has ancient roots. While men hunted and women nurtured, females developed a special connection. Women help each other to belong to themselves. Women have tended and befriended other women since the dawn of time. Shelley E. Taylor (2002) coined the concept *tending instinct* to designate a kind of female nurturing and relaxation response. Specifically, she defined tending as nurturing activities designed to reduce distress and promote safety in order to protect mother and child (Taylor et al., 2000). Moreover, Taylor (Taylor et al., 2000) identified befriending as the creation and maintenance of social networks that may aid in the reduction of distress. As discussed in the introductory chapter, when women engage in tending and befriending, they release female reproductive hormones (i.e., oxytocin) and an endogenous opiod peptide mechanism (Uvnas-Moberg & Petersson, 2005). A combined physiological and behavioral female bond shields women from isolation and provides them with solace.

The tending instinct has evolved since olden times into a sisterhood of the heart. Such a unique female connection imparts meaning to women's lives. In other words, women confirm, validate, and legitimize their close friends' feelings and experiences. As women find meaning in their lives, they increase their capacity to thrive. Research has confirmed that women enhance their intimate friends' happiness. A recent study showed that Australian women ranked their friends over their family, food, material goods, money, sex, and shopping as the greatest source of happiness (Shespot, 2010).

The aforementioned study's findings echo among many women. For example, African American women coined the term Sister/Friend to designate this special female bond. In this book, Thema Bryant-Davis eloquently described the healing role of Sister/Friends in the lives of African American women. Likewise, Carrie L. Castañeda-Sound, Lillian Comas-Diaz, and Louise Bordeaux Silverstein discussed the Latino female bond of *hermana de corazon y alma* (sister of the heart and soul) and *comadre* (co-mother) as a major support system among Latinas.

Certainly, the women psychotherapists in this anthology provided testimony to the power of women's intimate friendships. Simply put, these women explored the special connection of a sisterhood of the heart. The women psychotherapists came from different walks of life. They were young, middle aged, and older women; as well as White, African American, Latina, Asian American, Native American, and multiracial women. These feminist psychotherapists paid homage to women whose caring relationships fostered healing, empowerment, and transformation. The therapists identified a wide range of women as sisters of their heart. These women friends were relatives, peers, teachers, mentors, colleagues, employees, and even intellectual figures.

The narratives in this collection reflected how the contributors' intimate friends shaped their personal lives as well as their professional roles as feminist therapists. Most importantly, the women psychotherapists demonstrated how they incorporated their "sisterheart" wisdom into feminist therapy. Three major processes emerged in the women's reflections, namely, healing, empowerment, and transformation. Since the introductory chapter presented the healing effects of women's intimate friendships, this chapter discusses the empowering and transformative effects of women's close friendships. Moreover, it examines the incorporation of women's friendships principles into feminist therapy. This chapter concludes with a presentation of lessons learned from the perspective of intimate women's friendships.

EMPOWERMENT

> For women, the need and desire to nurture each other is not pathological but redemptive, and it is within that knowledge that our real power is rediscovered.
> – Audre Lorde, (1984, p. 1)

Women friends empower each other. When women become empowered, they increase their resilience and enhance their ability to thrive. As Audre Lorde (1984) affirmed, women rediscover their real power when they nurture each other. To illustrate this, research has documented that women help intimate friends to cope with adverse events by providing emotional support, help, and resources—in addition to helping them to engage in healthier life styles (Cohen, 2004). In other words, women help their intimate friends to practice self-care and self-nurture. At times, women friendships' empowerment derives from facing internalized oppressions. For example, Iva GreyWolf painfully disclosed how a betrayal within an intimate friendship uncovered her codependence, and resulted in her engagement in self-care and recovery.

Intimate friends help women to define themselves during developmental periods. As identity definers, women empower their close friends to cope with life challenges. The contributors in this collection recognized intimate friends who empowered them to cope with developmental milestones during childhood, adolescence, and adulthood. Additionally, they identified life challenges such as separation, moving, immigration, acculturation, loss/grief, among others. To illustrate, Carrie Castañeda-Sound identified a childhood *hermana de corazon y alma* (sister of her heart and soul) who helped her to negotiate a dual developmental challenge. Castañeda-Sound met her *hermana de corazon y alma* when she changed schools at age 12. Similarly, Pratyusha Tummala-Narra immigrated from India to the United States and found a sister friend who helped her to navigate cultural adaptation and to negotiate a bicultural identity. Likewise, Lillian Comas-Diaz acknowledged her sister of the heart, who helped her cope with cultural adaptation when she moved from the United States to Puerto Rico at age six.

Empowerment fosters women's self-efficacy, mastery, and agency (Dass-Brailsford, 2007). Moreover, it helps women to increase their access to resources, develop options to exercise choice, strengthen their support systems, affirm their gender and cultural strengths, foster self-healing, overcome internalized oppression, and engage in transformative actions (Comas-Diaz, 2012). As women empower their sisters/friends, they help women to recognize their intersecting contexts, accept their experience as valuable knowledge, acknowledge their perspectives in life, and rediscover their power.

The advent of the Women's Movement brought a new consciousness about women's friendships. Indeed, a woman-centered consciousness provided avenues for a female-to-female empowerment. A political sisterhood emerged to mirror women's special bond. Indeed, developing and maintaining close relationships with women became a powerful political act. For instance, women's friendships provide an impetus toward social change (Castaneda & Burns-Glover, 2008). Within this context, women's friendships served as an act of resistance against patriarchy and sexism. As an illustration, Pratyusha Tummala-Narra stated that her close friendship with a sister of her heart became an act of resistance, because everything was open for discussion. Certainly, feminism brought a validation of women's sisterhood as an empowerment and transformative relational bond.

Feminist therapy emerged as a reaction to the dissatisfaction with mainstream therapy and consequently, it proclaimed a gendered validated method to healing women (Brown, 2010). In this way, feminist therapists aim to empower women by promoting their development of a favorable comfort-distress balance, gender and cultural identity awareness, a sense of personal control and self-efficacy, effective problem-solving skills, competent use of assertiveness, effectual access to facilitate social, economic and community resources, gender and cultural flexibility, and socially constructive activism (Worell, 1993).

As feminism opened an avenue for women's awareness of their gender oppression, it nurtured women's accountability to each other. Such accountability promoted social activism. A feminist accountability and activism helped mainstream feminists to hear the voices of diverse women, particularly the voices of marginalized women. What is more, a feminism of color emerged to address the needs of marginalized ethnic minority women. Alice Walker (1983) coined the term *womanism* to legitimize the feminism of women of color, especially African American women. Additionally, Latina feminism—*mujerismo*—emerged to address the role of racism, sexism, immigration, biculturalism, neocolonialism, and xenophobia among Latinas and Latinos (Isasi-Diaz, 1994). Womanists and *mujeristas* commit to struggle against oppression, affirm their gendered cultural strengths, and promote collective social justice (Comas-Diaz, 2008). To illustrate this, many young womanists and *mujeristas* recognize the power of Sister/Friends in their social justice work. For instance, a group of young women of color—mostly sister friends and *hermanas del alma*—organized themselves into the Young Women United (YWU) (http://www.youngwomenunited.org/whoweare/whywedoywu.html). These young women of color share knowledge, support, and become accountable to each other. In this context, they engage in social justice actions for all people. In particular, these young women empower each other and rescue their gender and cultural strengths in order to become strong women of color. Equally important, they use creativity, self-healing, and spirituality to engage in revolution and transformation.

TRANSFORMATION

> No person is your friend who demands your silence, or denies your right to grow.
> – Alice Walker

Women's intimate friendships promote growth and transformation. The narratives of the psychotherapists in this anthology attest to the powers of transformation of women friendships. Indeed, women friendships seem to have an alchemical way of asserting the positive aspects of marginality. Ruth Hall and Michelle Fine (2005) presented the concept of positive marginality as they stated that living on the outside and on the inside creates both strength and resistance to dominant distortions of women's realities. Moreover, embracing a positive marginality allows women to author their own voice to write and re-write their own scripts, independent of the dominant culture's messages.

Following this reasoning, several contributors described how their intimate friendships transformed and "equalized" power differentials between the two women. For example, Jennifer Ruff identified a mentor as her sister of the heart. This mentor offered Ruff supportive encouragement, modeling, transparency, and spiritual connectedness. Ruff reflected that the mentoring became a reciprocal relationship since it enhanced both women's personal and professional lives. Similarly, Janice Crawford found a teacher-mentor who became a source of strength and love during her development as a therapist. Crawford's experience with her sister of the heart and mind developed into a mutual transformation. In this fashion, Louise Silverstein discussed her special bond with an immigrant low-income woman who helped Silverstein to raise her children. She discussed how they transformed an employer-employee fiduciary relationship into a sisterhood of the heart. The transformation of such an unequal power relationship into an intimate friendship taught Silverstein powerful lessons about disconnection, such as otherhood, poverty, immigration, and cultural differences. Additionally, she received lessons about connection, in the form of empathy, resonance, co-mothering, companionship, and growth.

The empathic connection present in intimate friendships provides another source for women's transformation. At times, this connection is similar to having a spiritual twin. For example, Lillian Comas-Diaz asserted that she felt like she had been with her sister of her heart "since the beginning of time." Indeed, a spiritual element appears to be a component of many sisterhoods of the heart. Iva GreyWolf identified a prayer partner—her mother's best woman friend—as a transformative force in her spirituality. Similarly, Michi Fu stated that her intimate women's friendships helped her to extend her therapeutic scope. That is, she accepted a woman client's invitation to pray with her during therapy. Such an experience culminated in a profound transformation for Fu.

Notably, the contributors in this anthology identified feminism as a vital force of transformation in their lives. For example, Laura Brown discussed how feminism and feminist therapy allowed her to develop the nurturing and loving network of women friends who enhance her life. She asserted that writing about feminism and feminist therapy taught her to value women in spite of her history of female horizontal aggression. Certainly, both Laura Brown and Iva GreyWolf were exposed to female relational aggression (Lamb, 2002). Within this framework, relational aggression is the offspring of internalized oppression. Brown's reflections illustrate how feminist awareness transforms internalized gender oppression into an appreciation of women's intimate friendships. Likewise, women who identify with a powerful father figure may experience the Athena complex, that is, the male identified woman (Bolen, 1984). Lamentably, the Athena complex embodies an internalized female oppression and requires the identification with the mother in order for women to integrate both feminine and masculine energies (Murdock, 1990). Conversely, intimate women friendships constitute an antidote against the Athena complex and an avenue for women's transformation.

In a different shade of feminism, Sherri Taylor, an African American early career psychologist, narrated how she adopted Audre Lorde, an African American poet warrior womanist, as her sister of the heart. Reading Lorde's writings, Taylor learned that a critical aspect of becoming a healing change agent is to bear witness. In this process, Taylor witnesses the chaos of women's lives so that they might find a way into the poetry of their experience. She learned that poetry "introduces the possibility for narratives of oppression to be transformed by moments of resistance and resilience" (p. 28).

Female intimate friendships foster women's transformation in diverse ways. Carrie Castañeda-Sound credited her *hermana de corazon y alma* with the development of her *mestiza* Chicana consciousness. This type of awareness affirmed Castañeda-Sound's cultural identity and deepened her cultural and gendered strengths—strengths that she uses as a feminist psychotherapist.

FEMINIST THERAPY WITH A WOMAN'S FRIENDSHIP PERSPECTIVE

> Walking with a friend in the dark is better than walking alone in the light.
> – Helen Keller

Conducting psychotherapy involves walking in the dark of women's psyche. What is more, feminist psychotherapists can learn from intimate female friendships to accompany their women clients in the dark. Along these lines, Laura Brown suggested that women intimate friendships and feminist therapy are parallel dances. Consistent with these notions, the contributors in this anthology expanded the scope of feminist therapy through the use of a woman's friendship lens. For instance, Carrie Castañeda-Sound introduced cultural elements present in her relationship with her sister of the heart into her therapeutic approach. For example, she identified the use of language in therapy. In a clinical case study, Castañeda-Sound demonstrated how she empowered a woman client through the modulated use of language. Additionally, she discussed the use of her client's folk belief system such as *limpia* (cleansing) and calling her soul back to complement her feminist therapeutic work. Needless to say, Castañeda-Sound learned several healing approaches from her sister of the heart. Similarly, Lillian Comas-Diaz shared a clinical case vignette where she applied a *mujerista* orientation to infuse folk healing and psychospirituality into her feminist therapy practice. Specifically, she used a *comadre* approach—inspired by her sisterhood of the heart—to her feminist healing

Sherri Taylor learned from her sister of the heart that oppressed women need to reconnect with their embodied experience in order to obtain psychological healing. In this vein, Taylor allowed her embodied knowledge to supplement and inform her therapeutic interventions which facilitate women's (re)connection to their own embodied experience. According to Taylor, "embodied knowledge exists in a deep place of spirit, memory, and desire, and it produces the type of clarity and insight that willfully speaks truth to power" (p. 30). In this way, Taylor observed that therapeutic change is a reciprocal force between women therapists and women clients.

Similarly, Thema Bryant-Davis observed that her Sister/Friend connections represent a safe place, a truth telling place, and a healing place, where both women do and process the layered events of their lives. Such a healing process in women's friendships echoes the healing process of feminist psychotherapy. Interestingly, several women psychotherapists acknowledged the importance of creativity in healing, as well as in psychotherapy. For example, while Sherri Taylor reported using poetry in psychotherapy, Michi Fu commented that she utilizes art and music therapy in her work with traumatized women clients. These women psychotherapists agreed with Bohart (2013), who affirmed that creativity heals broken hearts. It appears that intimate women friends and feminist therapists choreograph similar dances. In summary, reciprocity, transparency, solidarity, mutuality, truth telling, authenticity, and creativity constitute SisterHeart attributes. Women psychotherapists may consider integrating these qualities into their feminist practices.

SISTER/HEART LESSONS

> Every one has a gift for something, even if it is the gift of being a good friend.
> – Marian Anderson

Sister/Friends help women to endure life challenges and encourage them to celebrate their victories in life—no matter how small or big they are. In this fashion, women may require different kinds of good friends to keep healthy and to maintain a sense of wellbeing. To achieve these goals, Prevention.com (http://www.prevention.com/health/sex-relationships/8-friends-every-woman-needs) advised women to have: 1) childhood friends who remember who their friend was before she became a woman; 2) new friends who connect the woman to other social networks; 3) a workout friend who will support their friend's physical activities; 4) a spiritual friend who accompanies the woman to yoga, meditation, prayer and other mindful activities; 5) a younger friend who can become the woman's mentee; 6) partner's friends because they help the woman's romantic relationship; 7) the mother—because 80% of adult women report having a strong mother-daughter bond (Fingerman, 2001); and 8) herself, because women need to love themselves the same way they do other important people in their lives.

Dovetailing these suggestions, the contributors in this anthology identified diverse women intimate friendships throughout their life. To illustrate, while Carrie Castañeda-Sound, Lillian Comas-Diaz, and Pratyusha Tummala-Narra discussed their childhood sister of the heart, Thema Bryant-Davis and Louise Silverstein regaled readers with stories about their women intimate friends during their adulthood. Moreover, Iva GreyWolf explained the importance of a sister of the heart who was her spiritual partner. Furthermore, Jennifer Ruff and Janice Crawford narrated stories about how a mentor and a teacher became sisters of their hearts. Finally, Michi Fu exhorted readers to "make new friends, but to keep the old."

In summary, conducting feminist therapy with a woman's intimate friendship perspective entails considering the following SisterHeart lessons:

- Value the gift of women friendship
- Tend and befriend
- Bear witness to women's pain and joy
- Ask for help—she will respond
- Transform oppression into resistance and resilience
- Practice healing and self-healing
- Engage in self- care
- Nurture women's growth
- Enhance women's ability to belong to themselves
- Enjoy the fruits of positive marginality
- Learn from connections and disconnections
- Forgive yourself and learn to forgive others
- Get out of your "head" and focus on your "heart"
- Heal with a thinking heart
- Reclaim your body
- Dare to be creative

CONCLUSION

In my friend, I find a second self.
– Isabel Norton

Intimate women friendships enhance each other's self-esteem, health, longevity, and happiness. The chapters in this book articulated a wealth of wisdom that readers can resonate with. These stories depicted the supremacy of women's close friendships. Moreover, they illustrated how sisters of the heart improve women's emotional, physical, and spiritual wellbeing. The women psychotherapists' reflections demonstrated how a unique female intimate friendship imparts meaning into women's lives. Simply put, a sister of the heart helps women to give birth to each other. Even more, a sister of the heart becomes a woman's second self.

REFERENCES

Anderson, M. *Every one has a gift for something, even if it is the gift for being a good friend.* Retrieved on November 19, 2012 from: http://www.goodreads.com/quotes/52500-everyone-has-a-gift-for-something-even-if-it-is

Bernikow, B. *Female friendships that work are relationships in which women help each other to belong to themselves.* Retrieved on December 12, 2012 from: http://quotepixel.com/author/louise_bernikow

Bohart, A.C. (2013). Helping clients heal broken hearts. In M.F. Hoyt (Ed.), *Therapist stories of inspiration, passion & renewal: What's love got to do with it?* (pp. 24–35). New York: Routledge.

Brown, L.S. (2010). *Feminist therapy. Theories of psychotherapy series.* Washington, DC: American Psychological Association.

Bolen, J. (1984). *Goddesses in everywoman: Powerful archetypes in women's lives.* New York: Harper Collins.

Castaneda, D. & Burns-Glover, A.L. (2008). Women's friendships and romantic relationships. In F.L. Denmark & M.A. Paludi (Eds.), *Psychology of women: A handbook of issues and theories (2nd ed.)* (pp. 332–350). Westport, CT: Praeger Publishers/Greenwood Publishing Group.

Cohen, S. (2004). Social relationships and health. *American Psychologist*, *59*, 676–684.

Comas-Diaz, L (2008). *Spirita*: Reclaiming womanist sacredness in feminism, *Psychology of Women Quarterly*, *32*, 13–21.

Comas-Diaz, L. (2012). *Multicultural care: A clinician's guide to cultural competence*. Washington, DC: American Psychological Association.

Dass-Brailsford, P. (2007). *A practical approach to trauma: Empowering interventions*. Thousand Oaks, California: Sage.

Fingerman, K.L. (2001). *Aging mothers and their adult daughters: A study in mixed emotions*. New York: Springer

Hall, R. & Fine, M. (2005). The stories we tell: The lives and friendship of two older Black lesbians. *Psychology of Women Quarterly*, *29*, 177–187.

Isasi-Diaz, A.M. (1994). *Mujeristas*: A name of our own. Sisters struggling in the Spirit. In N.B. Lewis (Ed.), *A women of color theological anthology*. (pp. 126–138) Louisville, KY: Women's Ministries Program, Presbyterian Church (USA).

Keller, H. *Walking with a friend in the dark is better than walking alone in the light*. Retrieved on December 12, 2012 from: http://acrosstheuniverseandbeyond.wordpress.com/2011/03/22/walking-with-a-friend-in-the-dark-is-better-than-walking-alone-in-the-light/

Lamb, S. (2002). *The secret lives of girls: What good girls really do*. New York, NY: Simon and Schuster.

Lorde, A. (1984). The master's tools will never dismantle master's house. In A. Lorde *Sister outsider: Essays and speeches*. Berkeley, CA: The Crossing Press. Retrieved on December 12, 2012 from: http://lists.econ.utah.edu/pipermail/margins-to-centre/2006-March/000794.html

Murdock, M (1990). *The heroine's journey: Woman's quest for wholeness*. Boston: Shambhala Publications.

Norton, I. *In my friend, I find a second self*. Retrieved on December 12, 2012 from: http://blogs.iesabroad.org/lauren-kelly/in-my-friend-i-find-a-second-self-isabelle-norton/

Prevention.com. *8 friends every woman needs*. Retrieved on December 12, 2012 from: http://www.prevention.com/health/sex-relationships/8-friends-every-woman-needs

Shespot (2010, March 5). *Friends (not shoes!) the source of women's happiness*. Retrieved on December 12, 2012 from: www.shespotau.com/Australian-women-friends-and-happiness.html

Taylor, S.E. (2002). *The tending instinct: How nurturing is essential to who we are and how we live*. New York: Holt.

Taylor, S. E., Cousino, L., Klein, L., Lewis, B.P., Gruenewald, T.L., Regan A.R., Gurung, R. & Updegraff, J.A. (2000). Behavioral responses to stress in females: Tend and befriend, not fight-or-flight. *Psychological Review*, *107*(3), 411–429.

Uvnas-Moberg, K. & Petersson, M. (2005). Oxytocin, a mediator of anti-stress, well-being, social interaction, growth and healing (Abstract). *Z Psychosomatic Medical Psychotherapy*, *5*(1), 57–80.

Walker, A. (1983). *In search of our mothers' gardens: Womanist prose*. New York: Harcourt Brace Jovanovich.

Walker, A. *No person is your friend who demands your silence, or denies your right to grow*. Retrieved on December 12, 2012 from: http://www.goodreads.com/quotes/2574-no-person-is-your-friend-who-demands-your-silence-or

Worell, J. (1993, November). *What do we really know about feminist therapies: Approaches to research on process and outcome*. Invited Presentation. Austin, Texas: Texas Psychological Association.

Young Women United (YWU). Retrieved on July 18, 2012 from: http://www.youngwomenunited.org/mission/

Index